David Reff

# TWENTY-SOMETHING IN THE 1990s

*This book is dedicated to the founder of the 1958 and 1970 British Birth Cohort Studies, Neville Butler.*

# Twenty-something in the 1990s

## Getting On, Getting By, Getting Nowhere

*Edited by*
JOHN BYNNER, ELSA FERRI and
PETER SHEPHERD
*Social Statistics Research Unit of City University*

**Ashgate**
Aldershot • Brookfield USA • Singapore • Sydney

Published by
Ashgate Publishing Limited
Gower House
Croft Road
Aldershot
Hampshire GU11 3HR
England

Ashgate Publishing Company
Old Post Road
Brookfield
Vermont 05036
USA

**British Library Cataloguing in Publication Data**
Twenty-something in the 1990s : getting on, getting by,
   getting nowhere
   1.Young adults - Great Britain - Social conditions 2.Great
   Britain - Social conditions - 1945 -
   I.Bynner, John, 1938- II.Ferri, Elsa III.Shepherd, Peter
   305.2'42'0941'09049

**Library of Congress Cataloging-in-Publication Data**
Twenty-something in the 1990s : getting on, getting by, getting
   nowhere / editors, John Bynner, Elsa Ferri and Peter Shepherd.
       p.    cm.
   Includes index.
   ISBN 1-84014-014-3 (hardcover)
   1. Young adults--Great Britain--Economic conditions--Longitudinal
studies. 2. Young adults-Great Britain--Social conditions-
-Longitudinal studies. I. Bynner, John.  II. Ferri, Elsa.
III. Shepherd, Peter.
HQ799.8.G7T95 1997
305.235'0941--dc21                                        97-30130
                                                            CIP

ISBN 1 84014 014 3

Cover designed by Kevin Dodwell
Printed and bound by Athenaeum Press, Ltd.,
Gateshead, Tyne & Wear.

# Contents

# List of Tables

# List of Figures

# Acknowledgements

The origins of the survey of 26 year-olds, on which this book is based, go back to 1970; in that year the third of Britain's internationally renowned birth cohort studies was launched. The 1970 British Birth Cohort Study (BCS70) followed similar studies of perinatal mortality begun in 1946 and 1958. Each comprised all births in a single week in Britain - in the order of 17,000. Neville Butler was instrumental in setting up the 1958 and 1970 birth cohort studies; it was also his foresight which was instrumental in their continuing as longitudinal studies through childhood and adolescence into adulthood. Taken together, the British birth cohort studies represent a remarkable research resource unequalled in any other country.

We are grateful to the Economic and Social Research Council who funded the survey. We also acknowledge with thanks the continuing support of the International Centre for Child Studies, under the directorship of Neville Butler, who were responsible for BCS70 until it came to the Social Statistics Research Unit at City University in 1991. The MORI research organisation carried out the survey in April 1996, at the time of the cohort's 26th birthday, and prepared the data collected for analysis. The cohort members' response to the questions asked them was magnificent. We are most grateful to every one of them who took the trouble to fill in our questionnaires; the data they supplied have enabled us to construct this unique picture of a generation.

To ensure that the findings of the survey were published as soon as possible after the survey, there has been great pressure in the production of this book. Gratitude is due to everybody in SSRU who contributed much time and effort to getting it out on time. Kate Smith and Kevin Dodwell produced the final versions of the graphics and tables for the book. Kate Smith produced the pen portraits of cohort members presented in Chapter 7, assisted authors in accessing the database and helped with data analysis. Mahmood Sadigh managed the computing resources for the project. Kevin Dodwell, Denise Brown and Mary Ukah, with the help of other staff, coded the data needed for analysis. Sheila Young did much of the typing, helped by Theresa Carey. The dedication of everybody involved in the project was essential to its success.

Finally, the chapters were written by a number of SSRU staff and other colleagues, working together in a team to ensure a coherent approach to the data analysis and writing. Responsibility for the final version of the manuscript lies with the editors.

John Bynner, Elsa Ferri, Peter Shepherd.

# 1 Changing Lives in the 1990s

JOHN BYNNER, ELSA FERRI and PETER SHEPHERD

## Introduction

This book is about the lives, past and present, of 9000 young adults who were all born in the same week of 1970. A generation born in that year has grown up in quite different circumstances from one born even a decade earlier. The 70s and, particularly, the 80s in Britain were periods of massive social, economic and political transformation. The standard transition from school to work, which up until the end of the 1960s two thirds of young people made at the age of 16, was replaced ten years later by one in which only one third were leaving school at the minimum age. And most of those who did leave then went into training schemes rather than jobs.

Our cohort born in 1970 were, at 16, still leaving education in large numbers - less than half were staying on - but they faced a labour market where youth employment was fast disappearing. In place of jobs were a variety of training schemes brought together by the Government's Manpower Services Commission, under the general heading of the Youth Training Scheme (YTS). As social security benefits were still available to young people at the time - they were terminated in 1988 - unemployment was also an option. The lucky ones - mainly in the south of England - got the few jobs that were still available to young people.

*Changes in the labour market*

The origins of these transition problems are not difficult to see. With the advent of computer-based information technology, the nature of employment had been rapidly transformed. Much unskilled work in manufacturing had disappeared, and new kinds of skill were increasingly in demand from employers. Coupled with the economic recessions of the early 1980s, and with fierce competition from the rapidly growing economies of Asia, manufacturing industry collapsed, and the traditional industrial heartlands of Britain experienced unemployment on an unprecedented scale.

Early Government attempts to combat youth unemployment, such as the Youth Opportunities Programme (YOPs), were premised as much on a perceived need to keep young people off the streets, as on a commitment to promoting and facilitating fundamental changes in their employability. In 1981, a Government White Paper, the *New Training Initiative*, heralded a quite new approach, whereby the new technological skills that industry was now demanding would be supplied to potential employees through training schemes. These replaced the traditional apprenticeships, which tended mainly to be done by boys, and had been seen for some time to be getting increasingly out of date, typically being labelled as 'time serving'. Youth training in the 80s, directed at the whole annual cohort of 600,000 school leavers, went though a variety of forms, before it finally terminated in 1988 as a national scheme, and was handed over to the locally based Training and Enterprise Councils (TECs). In 1994, yet another development was announced, the modern apprenticeship, which re-established the traditional means of training young people for jobs, but through a much shortened two year period of work- based training combined with education.

The whole training initiative heightened awareness of the need for 'up-skilling' the population, and extended into the education system itself. The National Council for Vocational Qualifications (NCVQ) was set up in 1988 to rationalise the myriad vocational qualifications that had been offered until then, and a national curriculum was established in Britain for the first time, in which 70 per cent of the subject matter taught in schools was laid down by Government.

These British labour market initiatives cannot be seen in isolation from a worldwide transformation of economies, and the ways of producing goods and services and generating wealth. The defining feature of these globalising pressures is one of accelerating technological change. For the worker, however, its main consequence is felt in terms of ever-increasing uncertainty and risk (Beck, 1986). In place of the standard patterns of entry to adult life dictated by such structural factors as class, gender, ethnicity and locality, for a generation born in 1970 the routes to adulthood were becoming more *individualised*. Young people were having to 'navigate' their way through a range of education, training and early employment options, trying all the time to insure their future against the risk of short-term or continuing unemployment (Evans and Furlong, 1997). The consequence was a general extension of the transition to employment, with a moratorium on full-time permanent work extending well into the twenties for large numbers of young people.

To find their secure niche, or series of secure niches, in the labour market, young people were under increasing pressure to acquire qualifications and a range of new skills, to make them attractive to employers. This meant that those who failed to acquire these elements of 'human and social capital', became increasingly *marginalised*. The financial journalist Will Hutton refers to '30/30/40' societies, in which as much as 40 per cent of the population are permanently in a half-way house of casual jobs or continuing unemployment (Hutton, 1995). The title of this book tries to encompass this new stratification of Britain based on job security and prospects: 'Getting on, Getting by, Getting nowhere'.

*Family and social policy*

But it is not only changes in the economy and in the labour market which impacted upon those born in 1970. Increasing polarisation in advanced industrial societies challenged every element of family life and citizenship. The instability and insecurity which characterised the world of work were echoed in the personal and social domains. Relationships based on choice and emotional commitment were becoming both more diverse and more transitory. New patterns of shared living, family formation and family structures challenged traditional concepts of adult partnerships, parenthood and family life. Living together before marriage, and prior to having children, was becoming the norm. The increasing fragility of adult partnerships - whether cohabitations or marriages - was resulting in growing numbers of children being brought up in single parent households, or in often complex new family settings involving step-parents and step-siblings.

In the area of social policy, the election of the Conservative government under the leadership of Margaret Thatcher began a steady process of privatisation in the fields of education, health and welfare. This has introduced the concept of market forces as pivotal into many areas in which the principle of public service, embodied in the Welfare State, had become more or less taken for granted. The result has been an erosion of communal responsibility for providing, or guaranteeing, social and economic welfare, with increasing emphasis laid on individual responsibility in coping with hardship. For those without the resources to shoulder such responsibility, for themselves, their families and their dependent children, there is a clear threat to their welfare and well-being, and their ability to participate fully in the new social order. Universal provision has given way to the need for 'safety nets' and targeted help - drawing even more attention to the dependency of those relying on them. At the same time, sustaining unemployment at levels unthinkable in the two decades following the war places a continuing tax burden at ever-increasing levels on those in work. Middle class reactions to this - tax revolts - from California to Sweden have added to the political tensions - drawing out in starker contrast than perhaps ever before the difference between the solutions offered by the corporatist, broadly social democratic solutions of Western Europe, and those of US-inspired free market capitalism. The latter's manifestation in the 'politics of contentment' (Galbraith, 1992) is challenged by the growing problems associated with disadvantage, poverty and crime.

*Identity, lifestyle and politics*

Other changes were occurring in the ways young people formed their adult identities. In leisure life, they came under pressure, especially through the mass media, to adopt a lifestyle and identity shaped increasingly by their role as consumers rather than as producers - the dominant influence of the past. In place of the adult workplace and the occupations that went with it, attitudes, values and norms were informed increasingly by television and the other media. The role of parents as arbiters of behaviour became replaced by the peer group. Broader issues associated with lifestyle also arose in connection with health - with sexually transmitted diseases such as Aids, as well as drug and alcohol-related problems, casting a shadow over the whole decade of the 1980s. At the same time 'healthy living' became a clarion call with the major 'Health of the Nation' initiative, established in 1992.

Inter-group hostility and conflict, especially directed at ethnic minorities, was another growing, if not new, menace throughout this period. The mobility of populations, brought about by the political upheavals in Eastern Europe, was accompanied by increasing signs of emergent fascism, to which young people in Britain were not immune. At the same time, these worrying developments need to be set against counter trends, such as the vehement anti-racism, and commitment to new political programmes such as the Green movement, which were also prominent, especially among the young. There were signs that the traditional Party allegiances passed on from parents to children were losing their salience, with issue-based politics - ranging from anti-roads protests to animal rights - attracting allegiance instead (Banks et al., 1992). Set against these varying signs of 'new politics', however, was the other dominant feature of the period - apathy towards the political process and cynicism about politics and politicians, concentrated particularly among the less educated (Bynner and Ashford, 1994).

Another area where passions ran particularly high was the relations between the sexes. The politics of feminism, which dominated much of the 80s, transformed the way young women, particularly, saw their roles. Their subsequent better resilience to labour market changes, their move away from traditional 'female' subjects at school, and their heightened career aspirations were said to have produced a 'genderquake' (Wilkinson, 1994). But, as we show in this book, how far such shifts in male-female relations impacted on all areas of life, especially at home, remains much more debatable. At the time the young women born in 1970 were facing these choices, the great majority of women were still mixing family care and (part-time) work through a part of their adult lives, and were taking on most of the domestic responsibilities at home in a way still unknown to the vast majority of men.

*Themes of the book*

This brief summary of the changing context of the lives of our cohort born in 1970 helps to define the main themes of the book. We focus in particular on *polarisation*, *social exclusion* and *individualisation*, as manifested in the key life domains of these young adults: education, employment, family, health and values. In many instances, the findings from earlier birth cohort studies provide a back-cloth against which to set this evidence of change. Although much of the work that will subsequently be undertaken with the new data reported here will be designed to exploit its full longitudinal features, our concern in this book is to draw attention to the *here* and *now*. The evidence presented in the following chapters suggests that quite dramatic changes have occurred in the lives of the cohort members along the lines indicated above. Compared with a cohort born just 12 years earlier, their adulthood promises to be a much more challenging and difficult one. Great opportunities and successes are evident for some, while disadvantage, poverty and exclusion are the experience of others.

Before turning to the findings of the investigation, the remainder of this chapter presents an account of the history and background of the longitudinal birth cohort study which furnished the information. Brief reference is also made to two earlier cohort studies which, together with the 1970 British Cohort Study, make this country a world leader in the production and exploitation of these uniquely rich resources for research in the social sciences.

## The 1970 British Cohort Study

The 1970 British Cohort Study (BCS70) is one of three birth cohort studies that have been undertaken in Britain in the last fifty years. The others are the 1946 National Survey of Health and Development, and the 1958 National Child Development Study. Each started as a study of maternity services and perinatal mortality, with a cohort comprising almost all births occurring nationwide in a target week in the respective years.    Each study has subsequently comprised further follow-ups at various ages.    Both individually, and in combination, they present unprecedented opportunities to investigate the forces and patterns that have shaped, and continue to shape, the lives of three overlapping generations living in Britain today. Details of the 1946 and 1958 studies are available in the many publications that have been based upon them (e.g., Butler and Bonham, 1963; Chamberlain et al., 1975; Davie, Butler and Goldstein, 1972; Douglas, 1964; Ekinsmyth et al., 1992; Ferri, 1993; Fogelman, 1976; Wadsworth, 1991). Until 1985, the National Child Development Study was run by the National Children's Bureau, and until 1991, the 1970 British Cohort Study by the International Centre for Child Studies. Subsequently, each study became the responsibility of the Social Statistics Research Unit (SSRU) at City University, which has managed them ever since. Over this period, continuing support has been provided by the Economic and Social Research Council (ESRC) and the International Centre for Child Studies (ICCS). Funders of the earlier surveys have included  ESRC, the Medical Research Council (MRC), government departments and agencies, and ICCS.

BCS70 began in 1970 when data were collected about the births and families of 17,198 babies born in England, Scotland, Wales and Northern Ireland in the week 5th-11th of April. Four follow-ups since then have gathered information on the full cohort at ages 5, 10, 16 and 26. In 1975 and 1980, the sample was augmented by the addition of immigrants to Britain who were born in the target week in 1970. Subjects from Northern Ireland, who had been included in the birth survey, were dropped from the study in all subsequent sweeps.

The scope of enquiry broadened from a strictly medical focus at birth, to encompass physical and educational development at the age of five. Social development was added at ages 10 and 16, and further extension at age 26 covered labour market experience, adult relationships and social attitudes. In 1992, a sample survey of 1,650 cohort members was undertaken by SSRU, to investigate the forces and circumstances which influence young people in their transition from full-time education to employment, and to examine the extent of literacy and numeracy problems in the cohort (Ekinsmyth and Bynner, 1991; Bynner and Steedman, 1995). The purpose was to find out what underlay these problems, and how they affected employment and activity in other areas of life. In addition, this survey was designed to serve as a feasibility study for a full sweep of the cohort in their early twenties.

Over the years, data have been collected from different sources and by various instruments. In the birth survey, a questionnaire was completed by the midwife present, and supplementary information obtained from clinical records. In 1975 and 1980, parents of the cohort members were interviewed by health visitors, and information gathered from head and class teachers (who completed questionnaires), the school health service (which carried out medical examinations on each child), and the subjects themselves (who undertook tests of ability). In 1986, sixteen separate survey instruments were employed, including questionnaires completed by parents, class and head teachers, and medical examinations. The cohort members completed questionnaires, kept two four-day diaries (one for nutrition and one for general activity), and undertook educational assessments.

The most recent follow-up, which provided the material for this book, was carried out by means of a postal survey in 1996, when the cohort members were 26 years of age.

The opportunity to conduct this new sweep arose through a grant from the ESRC. The sum available was limited and had to be used over a fairly short time period. In consequence, all the detailed preparations, including consultations over the development of the questionnaire, and the tracing of cohort members, had to be carried out in a few short weeks. Nevertheless, from the response obtained and the rich data collected, we are confident in the success of the survey. It has established excellent foundations for a continuing programme of research throughout the lives of the cohort members.

*Questionnaire development*

The postal questionnaire used for the survey was developed by the cohort studies research team at SSRU, in consultation with those who had been involved with the design and analysis of earlier BCS70 sweeps, and those familiar with the 1958 National Child Development Study (NCDS). It was based on survey instruments used for the 23 and 33-year NCDS follow-ups and the BCS70 1992 Sample Survey, and was designed to provide details of the views and current circumstances of the cohort member in a number of key areas, plus more limited information on their experiences since the last follow-up in 1986. Successive drafts of the questionnaire were piloted on groups of young people of approximately the same age as the cohort members. The final 16-page version included questions concerning: qualifications and skills; training; employment and earnings; unemployment and periods out of the labour market; relationships, marriage and children;

housing and household; health and health-related behaviour; and the views of cohort members about topics such as law and order, politics, jobs, and marriage and family.

*Tracing*

The continued success of longitudinal studies like BCS70 is dependent upon knowing the whereabouts of the study subjects. For the purposes of the follow-ups in 1975, 1980 and 1986, the cohort members were traced mainly through schools, and no effort was made to maintain contact in the intervening years. Following the 1986 survey, it was no longer possible to trace the 16,000 cohort members anew in this way. Efforts were made to maintain contact with as many as possible by mailing an annual birthday card to those for whom a current address was still available. This card was designed to give cohort members information about the study and to confirm address details and other helpful information. As a result of these efforts, information about the whereabouts of some 9,000 of the 16,000 cohort members was available at the time that preparations for the 1996 follow-up began in January, 1996.

In an attempt to increase the number of current addresses available, a special tracing exercise was begun at that time. Several sources were pursued, including a postal screening of the cohort carried out as part of a study of inflammatory bowel disease by SSRU and the Royal Free Hospital, London. This collaboration also enabled both projects to benefit from an approach to the Driver and Vehicle Licensing Agency, who agreed to mail tracing letters to cohort members identified by them on their address database. Finally, towards the end of the limited period available, addresses for some untraced cohort members were identified in the address records of the Family Health Service Authorities in England and Wales, and the Health Boards in Scotland.

By the end of June 1996, the tracing exercise had produced information about the current whereabouts of an additional 4,500 cohort members, providing a total of some 13,500 potential respondents for the postal survey.

*Survey*

The survey itself took place between April and September, 1996. Questionnaires were mailed to all cohort members for whom a current address was available. This was undertaken by the MORI research organisation, who were responsible for the printing and distribution of questionnaires, the mailing of reminders, and the initial data entry and checking. Additional data checking and coding were undertaken by SSRU.


*Survey response and response bias*

Completed questionnaires were received from 9,003 cohort members - two-thirds of those to whom a copy was mailed. This is a very encouraging response, given that many cohort members were being contacted for the first time since 1986. Indeed, questionnaires were returned by 77 per cent of those mailed in the first batch, which was largely made up of those with whom contact had been maintained over the years. This suggests that future surveys may be more successful if contact can be maintained with all those newly traced. Using interviewers to conduct the field work is also likely to increase response.

Although a generally acceptable response rate has been achieved, anything less than a perfect response raises the question of whether those who completed a questionnaire are representative of the cohort. This issue has been explored by exploiting a possibility only available to longitudinal studies: comparison of the achieved sample - those cohort members who returned a questionnaire - with the target sample - the cohort at birth, and in subsequent follow-ups.

We have made a large number of comparisons between the achieved sample and the target sample. They take the distributions of selected variables covered in the earlier BCS70 follow-ups and of the same variables in the sample still participating at age 26. The variables chosen cover such areas as education, social and economic circumstances, financial problems, the family and relationships, housing and household, and health. Encouragingly, this analysis reveals that the achieved sample does not differ greatly from the whole cohort as it was at birth. Although it appears that men, and those who experienced disadvantage in the areas identified above, are slightly under-represented in the 1996 follow-up, the differences are small. It seems we can be confident that the findings from the survey reported here can be regarded as truly representing the experiences of the 1970 birth cohort as a whole. For the future it means that the cohort is in good condition for further follow-up and that the longitudinal data set as a whole is sound.

Further details of this analysis of differential response are provided in Appendix 1, together with additional information on the preparation, conduct and outcome of the survey.


## Presentation of findings

In analysing the survey data, we have focused on straightforward description of the cohort at age 26 - more in the nature of a snapshot of a generation than a detailed analysis of their lives. In later work, we plan to dig much deeper into the circumstances and experiences that shaped development from birth to 26. With the benefit of an interview-based survey that we also hope to undertake, we shall be able to draw on the detailed record of life events occurring since the cohort members left school.

The findings of the survey are presented in the following chapters, each of which examines the cohort members' experience in the different domains of life: education and qualifications (Chapter 2), employment (Chapter 3), living arrangements and family formation (Chapter 4), health and health behaviour (Chapter 5) and views and politics (Chapter 6). The book ends with some general conclusions - getting somewhere, getting nowhere in the 1990s (Chapter 7).

The findings help to amplify the themes identified at the beginning of this chapter, concerned with the changing nature of life in modern Britain. We see evidence of much achievement and fulfilment among some of our cohort members, not all of which is tied to the traditional influences of gender and class. At the same time, we identify individuals and groups whose lives appear to be marked by failure to achieve a successful transition to adult life. Evidence of their disadvantage in the labour market and at home, and their relatively poor physical and psychological state, points, in comparison with past generations, to an increasing gap between those who are succeeding and those who are falling behind. Our book serves, therefore, as something of a signpost to the uncertainties, and the problems associated with them, that are likely to dominate the next century's social and political agenda.

# 2 Getting on with Qualifications

JOHN BYNNER and SAMANTHA PARSONS

## Introduction

We hear a lot these days that 'education matters', but for the generations preceding that of the 1970 cohort, there was a relatively narrow view of what this meant. For the 1958 cohort, who reached the minimum school leaving age of 16 in 1974, two out of three left full-time education then, and by the age of 18, only one in eight was still actively involved. On the continent, education participation rates had been changing more rapidly. Although education beyond 18 continued to be largely the experience of an elite, many more young people on the 'non-academic' route stayed on beyond the minimum leaving age of 16 than was the case in Britain, becoming engaged in vocational education programmes based in the school, as in Sweden, or in the workplace, as in Germany.

In Britain, such a tradition of vocational education had never become firmly established: from the total cohort of 600,000 16-year-olds leaving school each year, only 120,000 ever entered apprenticeships at their peak, and only 20,000 of these were held by girls. The great majority of young people left school to move directly into a job. What work-related skills they subsequently acquired were largely what their first employers gave them. Day release (one day a week) was supposed to be the norm for such young workers. But what they did on the one day off was never properly absorbed into a vocational curriculum directly related to their work, and consequently was generally little valued.

In the mid 1970s, the situation began to change. New technology wiped out large areas of manufacturing industry in which the young school leavers had found employment, and a deepening economic recession added to the squeeze on jobs. Interestingly, with the rise of service industries, which also accompanied the down-turn in manufacturing, women's employment tended to be better protected. A study of young adults in four UK labour market areas, based on surveys of 18-23 year-olds conducted in the early 1980s, found that in the towns hit worst by recession, unemployment among young men had increased massively, whereas among young women retention of employment was much higher (Ashton and Maguire, 1986).

The transformation of the labour market brought about by these changes initiated a series of responses from Government. The first of these, the Youth Opportunities Programme (YOPs), sought an alternative to unemployment by giving young people work experience, though it was seen by many commentators as largely a measure for keeping unemployed youth off the streets (e.g., Bates et al., 1984). In 1981 the situation changed again, with a totally new approach to youth unemployment. The *New Training Initiative* heralded universal youth training for *every* school leaver, not just as an alternative to unemployment, but as a positive means of equipping him or her with the new skills that modern industry demanded. Initially a one year scheme, introduced in 1983 and by 1986 extending to two years, the national Youth Training Scheme (YTS), offered either by an employer or by the local community, comprised a programme of classroom-based vocational education and training, and work-based experience. Its outcome was a training certificate, or recognised vocational qualification, which at the time comprised the certification offered by BTEC (Business and Technical Education Council), CGLI (City and Guilds London Institute) and RSA (Royal Society for Arts). So confident was the Government that the scheme was better than other alternatives, that the four to five year apprenticeships, which the elite of young school leavers had entered in the past, were largely wound up and absorbed into an expanding YTS.

YTS seemed at the time to offer a means for Britain to approach continental standards of vocational education and training of the kind offered in Germany's famed 'dual system' - combining employment-based training with vocational schooling. In fact, in some respects, in its final post-1986 form, YTS could be seen as a British - albeit compressed - version of the German apprenticeship (Bynner and Roberts, 1991). The problem with it was that most young people who left school did so to get a job which paid full wages. What they got instead was training with an allowance - half the average youth wage - which was all that was offered on YTS. Hence, to most young people and their parents, YTS was always seen as an inferior kind of job, and most left the scheme they were on at the earliest opportunity. Moreover, the culture of employment in Britain, especially as dictated by employers' attitudes, failed to recognise vocational training as a distinct stage of life in between school and getting a 'proper job'. Many of the employers who offered YTS treated the young trainees as nothing more than cheap employees subsidised by Government. Consequently, the label 'slave labour', applied to YTS by many young people, was no more than a natural response to it (Bynner, 1991). In areas where the adult labour market was in difficulty, the end product of YTS was often not a job but unemployment, attracting another derogatory label - 'warehousing' - to the scheme (Banks et al., 1992).

Such perceptions did enormous damage to the credibility of the whole training enterprise. With Social Security benefits withdrawn from young people in 1988, unemployment was no longer a viable option for most, so the choice became either to stay at school or do the YTS. Rationally weighing up the situation, that employers tended to value academic qualifications more than vocational certificates in appointing people to jobs, the majority of young people opted for the former, and staying on rates began to rise. YTS, subsequently transformed into Youth Training, and offered locally through the Training and Enterprise Councils (TECs) established in 1988, gradually declined. The wheel went full circle with the introduction in 1994 of yet another form of vocational preparation, the 'Modern Apprenticeship' directed, in the Secretary of State for Employment's words, at 'the most able of our young people'. The rest, if they left school, had to make do with whatever youth training remained in their local area. This was subsequently to be 'purchased' with 'training credits', to which all school leavers were entitled.

## What was on offer in education?

The 1970 cohort were, in a sense, at the heart of these changes. They could still opt for unemployment, because when they became 16 in 1986 Social Security benefits were still available to young people without jobs. They could also opt for YTS or stay on at school. What was available to decide their choices? This cohort was the last year group to experience the divided general examination system of GCE (General Certificate of Education) 'O' levels and CSE (Certificate of Secondary Education). They could, therefore, take the lower grade CSE exam, only the top performance of which equated with GCE, or they could take GCE with a view to doing 'A' levels in the sixth form (GCSE came in a year later). In reality, the choice was less theirs than their teachers, who generally decided who was up to 'O' levels and who was not. At 16 they could also continue in education via a Further Education College, where a wider range of courses, including the traditional vocational ones (BTEC, CGLI and RSA), were available. The rationalisation of these qualifications was only just beginning to take place, with the establishment in 1988 of the National Council for Vocational Qualifications (NCVQ), whose task was to draw all vocational qualifications together into a single system of National Vocational Qualifications (NVQs).

In the 1970 cohort, we see the beginnings of the major trend that has followed ever since - choosing, out of the various options available to young people, the one of staying on at 16. Table 2.1 shows that just under one in two left education at or before 16 (49 per cent of men and 42 per cent of women). This compared with 62 per cent of men and 55 per cent of women who left full-time education at 16 in the 1958 cohort. Another notable feature was that a much higher proportion of the 1970 cohort participated in higher education.

**Table 2.1    Age men and women left full-time education**

|                   | All<br>% | Men<br>% | Women<br>% |
|-------------------|----------|----------|------------|
| Pre-16            | 2        | 2        | 2          |
| Age-16            | 43       | 47       | 40         |
| Post-16           | 25       | 20       | 29         |
| Post-18           | 11       | 11       | 11         |
| Post-21           | 16       | 16       | 15         |
| Still in education| 4        | 4        | 3          |
| n (100%)          | (8893)   | (4057)   | (4836)     |

Figures 2.1a and 2.1b elaborate the picture further, showing the percentages of men and women in the 1970 and 1958 cohorts who were still participating in education at age points between 16 and 26. A gap in the participation rates in the order of 12 per cent exists for both sexes up until the age of 21. By age 26, none of the 1958 cohort remained in education, but in the 1970 cohort three or four per cent were still involved.

Beside the general trend towards staying on in the 1970 cohort, the graphs differ slightly in shape for men and women in *both* cohorts, reflecting the different career patterns of boys and girls. Thus, more young women stayed on for a year after 16 than did boys, whereas more young men were involved in education post-18. The additional year in education for girls without academic aspirations provided the opportunity to take the one-year business studies courses that give entry to the clerical and secretarial kinds of jobs that large numbers of them favoured. Boys without academic aspirations tended to leave education at the earliest possible age. Although this pattern was still evident in the 1970 cohort, more of both sexes stayed on post-16, and more girls continued to higher education.

**Figure 2.1  Per cent in full-time education between age 16 - 26: comparisons between BCS70 and NCDS**

**a) Men**

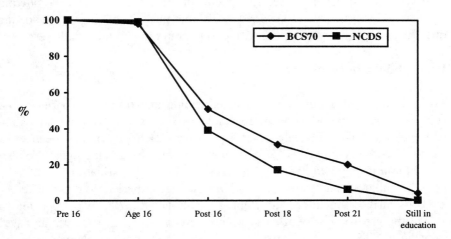

**b) Women**

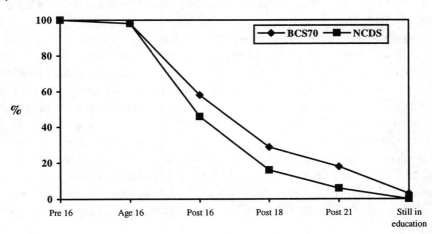

Interestingly, however, although more of the 1970 cohort stayed on at 16, the percentages of *both* cohorts who stayed on post-16, but had left by 18, was very similar: in the order of 20 per cent of men and 30 per cent of women. This suggests that the main shift in participation is firstly towards staying on post-16, and secondly, to continuing on to higher education. At the time the 1970 cohort was considering its post-16 options, the typical vocational route of staying on post-16 to do vocational qualifications and then leaving had not increased its appeal. In other words, increased staying on was still primarily concerned with the pursuit of higher academic qualifications, which in Britain still tend to count most with employers.

## Post-school education and training

To find out more about the kinds of education and training experience the cohort members had after leaving school at 16, we asked them whether they had ever attended YTS, any other government scheme, or had been on a training course lasting three days or more provided by an employer. We also asked them if they had done any courses leading to qualifications.

Table 2.2 shows the proportions who had experienced these different kinds of further education and training. At its height, YTS was expected to attract the great majority of early school leavers. In fact, just over half had been on a YTS scheme. Experience of other government schemes such as Employment Training (ET) was very rare: only one in twenty reported it. Employment-based training, and attendance on courses leading to qualifications, were more common, but still less than one-third of men and women had experienced either. A notable feature of the post-school education and training reported by the 1958 cohort was the strong gender bias toward men. As we might expect, far more men than women in that cohort did apprenticeships (54 per cent to eight per cent), but this difference extended to courses leading to qualifications and employer-based training. For example, 52 per cent of men, in comparison with 37 per cent of women between 23 and 33 had received training from their employers. Only traditional Local Authority adult education was engaged in more by women than men. As Table 2.2 shows, this gender bias had largely disappeared for the 1970 cohort. YTS, and courses leading to qualifications, were engaged in by only slightly more men than women and, similarly, there was only a slightly greater tendency for employer-based training to be experienced more by men.

**Table 2.2    Per cent who had attended training schemes or courses leading to qualifications by gender: all who left full-time education at 16**

|  | All | Men | Women |
|---|---|---|---|
|  | % | % | % |
| Youth Training Scheme | 54 | 55 | 52 |
| Other government scheme | 7 | 9 | 4 |
| Course leading to a qualification | 30 | 33 | 28 |
| Work-related training (from employer) | 29 | 33 | 24 |
| n (100%) | (3997) | (1980) | (2017) |

These figures suggest a quite dramatic change in women's relation to employment. Going on courses often depends on the initiative of the individuals concerned; work-based training is usually initiated by employers. The major emphasis of much of the vocationally-oriented education programmes in schools, such as the Technical and Vocation Education Initiative (TVEI) and the YTS itself, was on equal opportunities for young men and for young women. Although as we see in a later chapter, occupations remain heavily segregated by gender, at least at the level of vocational preparation and in-house training, the policy seems to have paid off. Women in the 1970 cohort were getting a fairer share of the government and employer investment in education and training than their predecessors had done.

**Qualifications and who gets them**

The 1970 cohort still confronted a qualifications system largely based on the conventional academic qualifications: GCE 'O level', 'A level' and their Scottish equivalents. They were the last cohort to take these before GCSE replaced them in England and Wales. The National Council for Vocational Qualifications was established only in 1988, so the National Vocational Qualifications, which this body launched, were still relatively rare.

Table 2.3 sets out the percentages of cohort members who had gained different kinds of academic qualification. At least one half had achieved the GCE 'O' level standard A - C; half of this proportion had subsequently gained 'A' levels (24 per cent). Again there were no marked differences between the sexes in these achievements; though recently girls have tended to overtake boys in the qualifications they achieve. Table 2.4 similarly shows the percentages of cohort members holding the different vocational qualifications. Almost half of all men and women did not have any such qualifications. But this time traditional gender differences emerged, with men having City and Guilds craft-based qualifications and women having Royal Society of Arts (RSA) typing and clerical qualifications.

**Table 2.3   Per cent of men and women with academic qualifications**

|  | All | Men | Women |
|---|---|---|---|
|  | % | % | % |
| No qualifications | 5 | 6 | 5 |
| CSE - grade 1 | 34 | 30 | 37 |
| CSE - other grades | 51 | 49 | 52 |
| 'O'Level - grade A-C | 51 | 50 | 51 |
| 'O'Level - other grades | 25 | 25 | 24 |
| GCSE - grade A-C | 9 | 7 | 10 |
| GCSE - other grades | 4 | 3 | 5 |
| 'A'Level | 24 | 24 | 24 |
| Scottish 'O'Grade - grade A | 6 | 6 | 6 |
| Scottish 'O'Grade - other grades | 2 | 2 | 2 |
| Scottish Standard Grade - grades 1-3 | 2 | 2 | 2 |
| Scottish Standard Grade - other grades | 1 | 1 | 1 |
| Scottish Higher Grade | 4 | 4 | 4 |
| Scottish Certificate 6th Year Studies | 1 | 1 | 1 |
| HE Diploma | 6 | 6 | 6 |
| 1st Degree (BA, BSc, BEd, etc) | 19 | 21 | 18 |
| PGCE | 2 | 1 | 2 |
| Post Graduate Degree (MA, MSc, PhD, etc) | 3 | 4 | 3 |
| Other academic qualifications | 21 | 18 | 23 |
| n (100%) | (9003) | (4102) | (4901) |

**Table 2.4    Per cent of men and women with vocational qualifications**

|  | All % | Men % | Women % |
|---|---|---|---|
| No vocational qualifications | 45 | 48 | 43 |
| NVQ - level 1 | 2 | 2 | 2 |
| NVQ - level 2 | 3 | 3 | 3 |
| NVQ - level 3 | 2 | 2 | 2 |
| NVQ - level 4 | <1 | <1 | <1 |
| NVQ - level 5 | - | - | <1 |
| NVQ - level 6 | - | - | - |
| NVQ - level unknown | 2 | 2 | 2 |
| RSA - stage 1 | 14 | 2 | 23 |
| RSA - stage 2 | 9 | 1 | 15 |
| RSA - stage 3 | 3 | <1 | 5 |
| RSA - stage unknown | 6 | 2 | 9 |
| Pitmans 1 (elementary) | 3 | <1 | 5 |
| Pitmans 2 (intermediate) | 2 | <1 | 3 |
| Pitmans 3 (advanced) | 1 | <1 | 2 |
| Pitmans - level unknown | 4 | 1 | 7 |
| Access course | 1 | 1 | 1 |
| City & Guilds - operative | - | - | - |
| City & Guilds - craft/intermediary/ordinary/part 1 | 9 | 14 | 5 |
| City & Guilds - advanced/final/part 2 or 3 | 8 | 13 | 4 |
| City & Guilds - full technological | <1 | <1 | <1 |
| City & Guilds - other | <1 | <1 | <1 |
| Insignia award of technology | - | - | - |
| City & Guilds - level unclear | 21 | 26 | 16 |
| JIB/NJC - craft/technician certificate | - | - | - |
| JIB/NJC - award unclear | - | - | - |
| ONC/OND (or SNC/SND) | 4 | 7 | 2 |
| HNC/HND (or SHNC/SHND) | 4 | 7 | 2 |
| TEC/BEC/BTEC - National General Certificate/Diploma | 2 | 3 | 1 |
| - Higher or Higher National Certificate/Diploma | 4 | 5 | 3 |
| - qualification unclear | 11 | 11 | 11 |
| Foundation course for technical/business qualifications | 1 | 1 | 2 |
| Other technical/business qualification - HGV/PSV, etc | 26 | 27 | 26 |
| Full professional qualification | 3 | 4 | 3 |
| Part of professional qualification | 4 | 5 | 4 |
| Nursing qualifications | 5 | 1 | 8 |
| Other vocational qualifications | 8 | 7 | 8 |
| n (100%) | (7740) | (3509) | (4231) |

For the purposes of finding out who gets academic or vocational qualifications, we needed to simplify the data in table 2.3 and table 2.4. Accordingly, the qualifications  listed in table 2.3 were grouped in terms of five 'standards' identified with the *highest* (academic) qualification achieved: no qualifications; CSE; 'O' level; 'A' level; higher qualification; degree (or higher). The qualifications listed in table 2.4 were similarly grouped in terms of NVQ standards. Highlighting the different educational experiences of the 1970 and 1958 cohorts, tables 2.5 and 2.6 show that not only were far *fewer* 1970 cohort men and women without any academic or vocational qualifications, but far *more* had attained a degree level qualification.

**Table 2.5  Per cent with academic qualifications: comparison of highest qualification achieved between 1970 cohort (BCS70) at age 26 and 1958 cohort (NCDS) at age 33 by gender**

| Academic qualification | All | | Men | | Women | |
|---|---|---|---|---|---|---|
| | BCS70 | NCDS | BCS70 | NCDS | BCS70 | NCDS |
| | % | % | % | % | % | % |
| None | 6 | 19 | 7 | 20 | 5 | 17 |
| CSE - grades 2-5 | 17 | 18 | 19 | 20 | 17 | 16 |
| 'O' Level / CSE - grade 1 | 41 | 39 | 38 | 36 | 43 | 42 |
| 'A' Level | 11 | 10 | 10 | 10 | 12 | 11 |
| Higher | 5 | 2 | 4 | 1 | 5 | 2 |
| Degree + | 21 | 12 | 23 | 14 | 19 | 11 |
| *n (100%)* | *(8399)* | *(10493)* | *(3801)* | *(5125)* | *(4598)* | *(5368)* |

**Table 2.6  Per cent with vocational qualifications: comparison of highest qualification achieved between  BCS70 (age 26) and NCDS (age 33) by gender**

| Vocational qualification | All | | Men | | Women | |
|---|---|---|---|---|---|---|
| | BCS70 | NCDS | BCS70 | NCDS | BCS70 | NCDS |
| | % | % | % | % | % | % |
| None | 45 | 66 | 48 | 47 | 43 | 58 |
| NVQ1 | 10 | 4 | 9 | 4 | 12 | 7 |
| NVQ2 | 20 | 14 | 16 | 17 | 23 | 16 |
| NVQ3 | 12 | 8 | 15 | 13 | 10 | 4 |
| NVQ4 | 12 | 9 | 12 | 19 | 12 | 15 |
| *n (100%)* | *(7740)* | *(10303)* | *(3509)* | *(5083)* | *(4231)* | *(5220)* |

Ever since the pioneering work of such writers as Jean Floud and James Douglas, family social class, as assessed from father's occupation, has been established as one of the most powerful predictors of educational attainment (Floud, Halsey and Martin, 1956; Douglas, 1964). Another element of the equal opportunities policies that were prominent throughout the 1970s and 80s was the goal of reducing this class differential. Figure 2.2 clearly shows that for the 1970 cohort, such policies were having only a limited effect. Two thirds of those cohort members with fathers in professional occupations (when they were born) had achieved a degree, compared with only four per cent of those with fathers in unskilled manual occupations. There was a steady rise in qualification level as the social class of the fathers' occupation varied from unskilled, through skilled, to managerial, and professional.

**Figure 2.2 Per cent with a degree at age 26 by father's social class at birth (1970)**

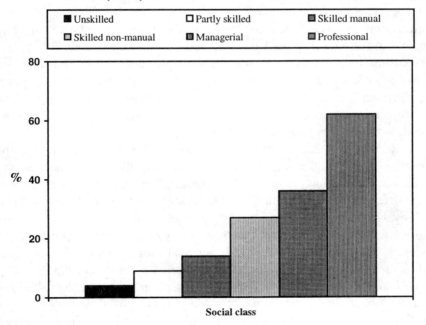

This family background factor was also strongly involved in the crucial post-16 transition: whether to stay on in education or leave. Over two thirds of young people coming from unskilled families, and just over half from skilled or partly skilled manual backgrounds, had left education by 16, compared with one tenth of those with fathers in the professions, and one quarter from managerial backgrounds.

This kind of relationship was also apparent over various indicators of disadvantage in the cohort members' own lives. Concentrating on those who left full-time education at 16, the group without any formal qualifications were far more likely to be renting, rather than buying, their homes, to be in a manual job and to have experienced a period of unemployment of at least two years.

Thus, despite all the attempts to improve educational opportunities across all social backgrounds, the figures show just how powerful the class structure, and its associated disadvantage, continues to be in relation to taking them up. Although some social mobility was evident, the acquisition of human capital (Becker, 1975) as embodied in educational qualifications remained predominantly with the middle class.

## Qualifications and the training experiences of early school leavers

Qualifications provide access to certain kinds of jobs. They also typically lead to further education and training and more qualifications. Many are prerequisites for advanced courses; for example, post graduate training is usually preceded by a degree, and a degree is usually preceded by 'A' level. Employers are also likely to invest more heavily in people with qualifications because they represent a 'good prospect' - i.e. the training will not be wasted. Is this true of early school leavers?

Restricting the sample to those who had left school at 16, the proportion of men and women without *academic* qualifications increased to 13 per cent for men and 11 per cent for women (from seven per cent and five per cent respectively). One-third had a CSE level qualification, over half had 'O' Levels. (The proportion of early school leavers without *vocational* qualifications slightly decreased for men - 46 per cent from 48 per cent; but increased from 43 per cent to 52 per cent for women). So how do qualifications relate to the early training experiences of this group of young adults? Table 2.7 gives clear support for the human capital precept that 'the more you have the more you get'. Men and women with 'O' Level qualifications were at least twice as likely as those without any qualifications to have received work-related training from an employer, or to have followed a course leading to a qualification (academic or vocational). Interestingly, men and women with CSE level qualifications were most likely to have participated in the Youth Training Scheme (61 per cent of men and 63 per cent of women). This compares with half of the men without qualifications and half of the men and women with 'O' levels. For women without qualifications the percentage dropped to 45 per cent.

This shows the kind of constituency of school leavers which YTS tended to pick up, confirming in certain respects young people's and their parents' prejudices about the scheme, and the voluminous criticism it attracted (for example, Bates, et al., 1984). The pick of the school leavers - those with 'O' levels - were recruited by employers directly into jobs. Most of those with minimal qualifications (CSE) found that YTS was the only labour market opportunity open to them. Most significant of all, though, were the prospects of those without qualifications at all. YTS was the most common activity for them after leaving school, but half did not even manage that. Women with no qualifications were the least likely group to have been on a YTS. With unemployment or unskilled work being the only other options, or in the case of women, early motherhood, their future prospects could only be described as bleak.

**Table 2.7**  **Per cent who had work-related training  or  had  attended courses  leading  to  qualifications  by  highest  academic qualification  at  26  and  gender:  all  who  left  full-time education at 16**

| Type of training | Men | | | Women | | |
|---|---|---|---|---|---|---|
|  | None | CSE | 'O'Level | None | CSE | 'O'Level |
|  | % | % | % | % | % | % |
| Youth Training Scheme | 51 | 61 | 50 | 45 | 63 | 54 |
| Qualification course | 15 | 28 | 40 | 12 | 21 | 33 |
| Work-related training (from employer) | 20 | 27 | 43 | 13 | 17 | 30 |
| n (100%) | (223) | (558) | (910) | (206) | (540) | (1006) |

The experience of training was also somewhat dependent on family situation for women, but not for men. Figure 2.3 shows that among the early school leavers, women with one or more children were far less likely to have had any work-related training than those who were childless. This was found at each qualification level. Postponement of child-bearing seems to be integral to employers having a positive view of their female employees.

**Figure 2.3  Work-related training from an employer compared for women with and without children: all women who left education at age 16**

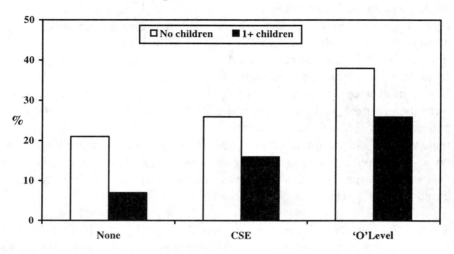

## Work related skills

In modern employment the core skills of literacy and numeracy are being supplemented by other 'generic' skills as essential prerequisites for getting a job. These include teaching skills, finance skills, use of computers and, increasingly, a wider range of numeracy skills than were required by employers in the past. The cohort members were asked to indicate how good they thought they were at a number of work-related skills, as shown in table 2.8. As we have found in other studies of skills based on the birth cohort studies (for example Bynner, Morphy and Parsons, 1996), the responses show striking gender differentiation. Thus, almost three quarters of the 1970 cohort women claimed to be good at writing clearly, compared with less than half of the men; whereas with respect to using tools, over half the men claimed to be good at this, compared with less than a third of the women. Other skills which differentiated the sexes were typing, using a keyboard, caring and teaching (all in favour of women), and doing mathematical calculations (in favour of men). Surprisingly, finance/ accounting skills were claimed equally by men and women, as were those involved in using a computer.

Table 2.8 also compares the proportions of the 1970 cohort who reported possession of these skills at 26 with those in the 1958 cohort at 33. The changing skills required by today's labour market is clearly reflected in the figures. Despite the 1958 cohort's seven year superiority in age at the time of the survey, a *higher* proportion of 1970 cohort men and women reported that they were good at writing, typing, using computers, doing maths calculations and (to a lesser extent) financial skills. Being good at using tools was reported by equal proportions of men and women in both cohorts. Reflecting their age and greater experience, good caring and teaching skills were more frequently reported in the 1958 cohort. Interestingly, despite the evidence we saw earlier of the success of equal opportunities initiatives in relation to access to courses and training, gender differentiation in the skills claimed was evident to the same extent in both cohorts. Only with respect to being good at mathematical calculations were there some signs that the gender gap was reducing.

**Table 2.8  Per cent reporting 'good' work-related skills: comparisons between 1970 cohort (BCS70) at age 26 and 1958 cohort (NCDS) at age 33 by gender**

| Skills | BCS70 | | NCDS | |
|---|---|---|---|---|
| | Men | Women | Men | Women |
| | % | % | % | % |
| Writing clearly | 47 | **72** | 39 | 60 |
| Using tools | **57** | 31 | 57 | 29 |
| Typing / using a keyboard | 30 | **46** | 14 | **28** |
| Using a computer | 36 | 38 | 20 | 17 |
| Looking after (caring for) people | 13 | **36** | 18 | **54** |
| Teaching | 25 | **37** | 32 | 43 |
| Mathematical calculations | **44** | 32 | **35** | 18 |
| Finance / accounting | 28 | 27 | 24 | 22 |
| n (100%) | (3984) | (4710) | (5239) | (5471) |

Note: Skills for which there are the largest gender differences (>10%) are shown in bold.

We would expect some of the skills shown in table 2.8, such as finance/accounting, to be either acquired mainly through work-based experience, or at least reinforced through employment. However, they also showed strong relationships to the qualifications held by the cohort members. Notably for men, the skills associated with highest qualifications were using a computer, keyboard skills, writing clearly, doing mathematical calculations, teaching skills and finance/accounting skills. Figure 2.4a and 2.4b highlight some of these relationships between highest academic qualification achieved and reported possession of skills for men and women separately.

Among men, the one skill associated with *lack* of qualifications was using tools: one and a half times the number of men with no qualifications claimed to be good at this, compared with those with degree level qualifications. For women, the same pattern applied with respect to 'caring' skills.

In other areas, the relationships were much the same for both sexes; that is to say, writing clearly, typing and keyboard skills, using a computer, teaching, using mathematical calculations and finance/accounting skills, were all positively associated with the level of qualification reached.

**Figure 2.4  Per cent reporting 'good' work-related skills by highest qualification at age 26**

a) Men

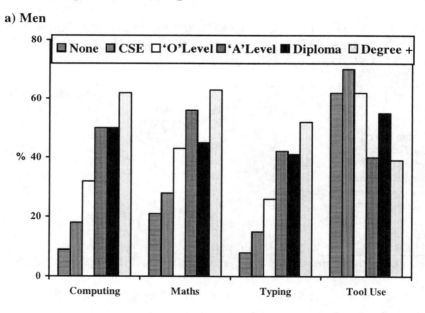

**Figure 2.4 continued**

**b) Women**

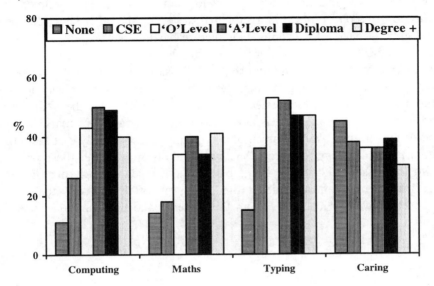

Notably, the skill which showed the strongest relationship to highest qualification was using a computer - particularly among the men. Nearly two thirds of men with degrees claimed to be good at using computers, compared with less than one in ten of those without qualifications.

Computing skills are, of course, central to obtaining and retaining jobs in large areas of modern employment. Thus, these figures point to the importance of extended education and higher level qualifications in acquiring such skills, either directly through education, or in the jobs to which extended education provides access. This supports the arguments of human capital theorists that investment in education pays dividends in terms of improved prospects later on. Skills may be seen as lying at the heart of job opportunities, through the access they give to particular kinds of job. This was reflected in the unemployment rates of people who were 'good' at each of the skills, compared with those who were 'poor' at them. Among people who had left school at 16, and reported 'poor' skills, unemployment rates were generally double those among people who claimed their skills were 'good'. For women, the category of part-time employment similarly showed a strong connection with poor skills - even among those who did not have any children.

The only skills that were associated with lack of qualifications were those which people at the bottom end of the labour market were likely to claim they were good at. Thus men in low status occupations claimed the ability to use tools. Women in a similar position, on the other hand, claimed to be good at caring for people. This picture has emerged repeatedly in our earlier studies. For example, in a sub-sample of the 1970 cohort at 21, similar (although weaker) relationships in the same direction were revealed (Bynner, 1996). This suggests that, as young people with poor educational attainments extend their experience of seeking employment, the skills they tend to develop become increasingly associated with the more marginalised kind of job. In the case of women, this typically signifies early exit from the labour market to have children. Thus, caring skills are the ones these women claim to possess. For men, the jobs on the fringes of Britain's largely unregulated building and decorating industry offer perhaps the main prospect of work. Hence the claim these men make that they are good at using tools.

**Conclusions**

The findings presented here give a mixed picture of improvements over some past failures in post-16 education and some continuing, if not worse, problems. Thus, the main success story emerging relates to the much wider opportunities available to young women for education and training after leaving school. The huge gap between the sexes revealed in the 1958 cohort was close to disappearing in the 1970 cohort, which suggests that the strident equal opportunities policies of the 1980s are now paying off.

Less satisfactory in equal opportunities terms is the evidence of the same gender differentiation in self-reported skills at much the same level as prevailed in the past. Young men and women saw themselves as being good at distinctively different sets of skills. This will inevitably point them in the direction of different sectors of the labour market, so gender segregation will remain. Clearly, this issue lies too deep in the psychological make-up of men and women, and especially in the attitudes of employers, to be resolved by improved access alone.

The promotion of post-16 education and training generally seems to have been effective in the sense that many more of the cohort members were staying on in education beyond the minimum age, and many more were engaged in some type of post-school training. The problem emerging was that some of this education and training experience - most notably the national Youth Training Scheme (YTS) - seemed to be serving a warehousing function as much as being a genuine ladder to a job. Thus, participation in it was dominated by young people with only basic qualifications. More young people with 'O' levels still managed to get jobs directly after leaving school.

Whatever its demerits, YTS provided some sort of meaningful activity for young people who would otherwise have been unemployed. This draws particular attention to the group without qualifications, who were just as unlikely to get involved in YTS as those with 'O' levels. It seems reasonable to assume that these young people had not passed up YTS for the better opportunity of a good job. Their marginalisation was almost invariably expressed through unemployment or peripheral types of work. Those with qualifications gained further from them through proficiency at more of the work-related skills. The key modern employment skill - computing - showed particularly strong connections with qualifications. Such findings also point to one of the dominant features of the modern age - growing polarisation and social exclusion. Those who have the foundations of success tend to get more and more opportunities to build on them. Those who start with least get left further behind. This will remain the major challenge facing the post-16 education and training system for the foreseeable future.

# 3   Life in the Labour Market

HEATHER JOSHI and PIERELLA PACI

## Introduction

Education lays the foundations not only for entry to the labour market in any kind of capacity but for the type of occupation entered. In a sample of 26-year-olds we would expect the great majority to have made the transition to employment in some form or another, and a large proportion would have been working since the age of 16. As we noted in Chapter 1, backed by evidence from the survey in Chapter 2, the relatively smooth transition from school to work of earlier generations was becoming less common for cohorts leaving school in the 1980s. Already, the availability of 'youth jobs' was becoming severely curtailed and many young school leavers entered the labour market via training schemes instead. As one of the last generations still eligible for social security payments (terminated for those under 18/19 in 1988), unemployment was another option. Already, the recognition of the need for qualifications to get any kind of reasonable job was growing. Also, staying on in education was coming to be seen as a better alternative to what was available in the labour market outside.

The early transition experiences paved the way for the kind of labour market participation in which the cohort members were engaged at 26. But the adult labour market they encountered was similarly undergoing periodic upheavals and more fundamental long term transformation. In place of the life-time employment within a particular occupation, often with the same employer, that many of their parents had experienced, the 1970 cohort members faced much more uncertainty about job security and prospects. Many were likely to find themselves on short term contracts, interspersed with periods of unemployment. Some relished the opportunity to try their hand at a variety of different kinds of work, before settling into something more permanent. These were generally the ones whose fund of human capital, acquired through education, was paying off. Others were operating more at the margins of the economy - doing all they could to find and retain any kind of job. How they responded to labour market opportunities and constraints was affected to a great extent by their family situation, which we consider in detail in the next chapter. Those with children were under particular pressure to maintain the flow of income, which only continuing employment could bring.

In this chapter, we see to what extent these broad social trends had affected the 26-year-olds' labour market participation. What was their experience of employment and unemployment? How was it related to their school attainment, subsequent vocational education and training, and family situation? Was their solution to the problem of employment essentially individualised - with marked evidence of social (and gender) mobility? Or were the old transition patterns based on class and gender holding up? Were some of the cohort exhibiting all the signs of success - as evidenced by high incomes and status - in what is now said to be a booming economy? Were others dropping through the net into possibly permanent marginalisation?

## Employment status at 26

At age 26, almost all the cohort members had made their move from education to the labour market. More than four out of five of them had a paid job: 87 per cent of the men and 80 per cent of the women (Table 3.1). This is comparable with the Spring 1996 national employment rate for men, but higher than that of women (68% for women aged 25-39) (DfEE, 1997).

Part-time employment was much more common among women than men, but even so, involved only one sixth of all women workers. The reverse applied with respect to self-employment: just over one in ten men were self-employed, compared with only four per cent of women.

Among the minority of the cohort not in work, the largest group (14 per cent) was women staying 'at home' to look after their families. Among the men without a job, unemployment was the biggest category, accounting for seven per cent. Very few women (four per cent) classified themselves as unemployed. These figures are only a little below the unemployment rates for 25-39 year olds in the Labour Force Survey for Spring 1996: nine per cent of men and seven per cent of women (DfEE, 1997). As the cohort's unemployment was well below the national rates of claimant unemployment at the time (11 per cent men of all working ages and four per cent women), it seems that these 26-year-olds were in a marginally more favourable employment situation than other age groups.

Very few cohort members described themselves as out of work due to a short-term health problem, or to being on a training scheme, and just three per cent reported themselves as 'still in full-time education'. Responses to other questions suggest that employment and education overlapped in some cases.

**Table 3.1    Current employment status at age 26**

| Employment status | Men % | Women % | All % |
|---|---|---|---|
| **Employed:** | **87** | **80** | **83** |
| full-time employee | 75 | 64 | 69 |
| part-time employee | 1 | 12 | 7 |
| self-employed full-time | 10 | 3 | 6 |
| self-employed part-time | 1 | 1 | 1 |
| **Not employed:** | **13** | **20** | **17** |
| unemployed | 7 | 2 | 4 |
| training scheme | <1 | <1 | <1 |
| short-term sick/disabled | <1 | <1 | <1 |
| full-time education | 3 | 2 | 3 |
| full-time care of home/family | <1 | 14 | 8 |
| long-term sick | 2 | 2 | 2 |
| **Total** | 100 | 100 | 100 |
| n (100%) | (4013) | (4736) | (8749) |

*Employment status and living arrangements*

The chances of someone, particularly a woman, being in paid work varied according to their domestic circumstances. Table 3.2 shows the proportions of men and women who were employed at age 26 by whether or not they lived alone, and if not, with whom. For women, further details are shown of whether employment was full- or part-time; those who said they looked after the home and family full-time are also distinguished from other non-employed women.

Relatively few of the 26-year-olds lived alone. Most of them, especially women, were living with partners, usually without any children. Most of those with children lived in two-parent families.

Among men, the employment rate was highest when they lived with a partner, and without children. Employment was lower among those living alone, living with others, or with parents. This suggests that, for some, unemployment may be an obstacle to forming one's own family, but having children relatively early may also be associated with labour market disadvantage, through pathways we can start to explore below.

### Table 3.2    Employment at 26 by living arrangements

| | | Lives alone | Lives with partner | With partner + child | No partner + child | With own parents | Lives with others | All |
|---|---|---|---|---|---|---|---|---|
| | | % | % | % | % | % | % | % |
| **Men** | | | | | | | | |
| | **Employed** | 81 | 95 | 88 | 93 | 84 | 83 | 88 |
| | n (100%) | (533) | (1262) | (696) | (19) | (1004) | (466) | (3980) |
| **Women** | | | | | | | | |
| | **Employed** | 86 | 95 | 52 · | 38 | 91 | 87 | 79 |
| | full-time | 82 | 88 | 22 | 17 | 84 | 84 | 66 |
| | part-time | 5 | 7 | 30 | 20 | 7 | 3 | 13 |
| | **At home** | 1 | 1 | 43 | 55 | <1 | 0 | 14 |
| | **Other** | 13 | 4 | 4 | 7 | 8 | 13 | 6 |
| | n (100%) | (351) | (1804) | (1135) | (288) | (776) | (364) | (4718) |

The women's employment rates showed some similarities and some contrasts with men's. First, in the large group living with a partner, but without children, employment was as high as for men in such couples (95 per cent). The presence of children was associated with dramatically lower employment rates, down to about a half for those in two parent families and below two fifths for lone mothers. More of their jobs were also part-time. These are patterns familiar from other national surveys (Ward et al., 1993). The lower employment rates of mothers were complemented by higher proportions giving domestic reasons for not being employed. Women living alone, with their own parents, or with others, had lower employment rates than those in childless couples, but notably they were *more likely* than men in similar circumstances to have a job. Women without partners or children reported marginally more unemployment than other women, but far below the average for men.

*Partners and earnings*

More than half the cohort were living as a couple. Was their partner also an earner, was only one half of the couple earning, or did neither of them earn? Figure 3.1 shows the different kinds of partnerships in terms of whether one or both partners was in full-time or part-time work, or unemployed.

## Figure 3.1 Earners in partnerships

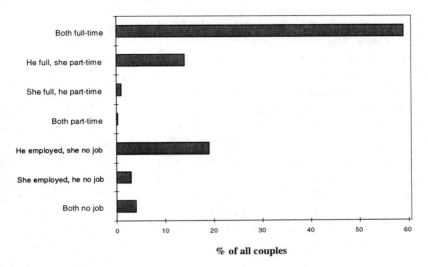

% of all couples

The largest group was two-earner couples: in three fifths of the couples, both partners had full-time jobs. This was followed by cases where the second earner was a woman in part-time employment - a common arrangement in Britain (Ferri and Smith, 1996). There were barely any cases where a part-time partner living with a full-time employee was the man, and couples in which both had part-time jobs were also extremely rare. Notably, the traditional male *sole* breadwinner pattern accounted for only one fifth of these young couples. 'Role reversal', where the women was the sole earner, occurred in three per cent of cases, but this was probably because the man was temporarily unemployed, or engaged in prolonged study, rather than a sign of the emergence of 'New Man' in the form of a 'househusband'.

In only one in 25 couples were neither of the partners earning. In this respect, the cohort resembles couples of other working ages, where the chances of access to the labour market polarise between zero-earner and two earner households (Gregg and Wadsworth, 1996). The human capital vested in qualifications appeared to be a factor in this. The better qualified cohort members tended to be in the two full-time earner couples, and the least qualified were over-represented in the no-earner partnerships. This would tend to widen the gap between the at least average earnings which the 'dual earner no kids' group could expect to command and the state benefits on which the jobless couples could be presumed mostly to depend.

*Employment status and qualifications*

The previous chapter has shown how the 1970 cohort were caught up in a rising wave of education and training provision. How far had their educational attainment affected their chances of having a job at age 26? Table 3.3 shows, for men, only employment rates; for women, it gives more detail of their position with respect to the labour market, distinguishing full and part-time jobs, and domestic from other reasons for not having a job. Since parenthood makes very little difference to men's employment, only the women are subdivided into those with and without children in the home.

For men, employment rates rose as qualifications increased from none or minimal to 'O' and 'A' levels. Only two thirds of those with no qualifications had jobs. Men in this category also had the highest rates of unemployment as well as of long-term sickness (not shown in the table). At the other end of the scale, the employment rate of men with degrees, at 86 per cent, dropped just below the 90 per cent level for those with qualifications at 'O' level or better, largely because eight per cent of them were still in full-time education.

Women, taken as a whole, displayed a steeper rise in employment rates with increasing levels of education. This is largely because the less qualified women were more likely to have acquired family responsibilities by age 26. Consider the women who (as yet) had no children: their employment rates followed a similar pattern to men's, although they were, in fact, consistently higher (92 per cent overall against the men's 88 per cent). Unemployment was generally low, with little significant difference by qualification level. The least qualified childless women were slightly more likely to be in part-time jobs than those with more qualifications. Among graduates, six per cent were still in full-time study.

Nearly one in three of the women had children living with them at the time of the survey. They had lower levels of qualifications, and substantially fewer of them were likely to be employed than childless women. This in itself could account for the gradient by qualifications in their employment rates. But there were also differences *within* the group of mothers. Full-time employment rates rose steadily with level of qualifications, from just one in ten of those with no qualifications to nearly one half among the graduate mothers.

**Table 3.3  Employment at 26 by highest qualification, gender and women's responsibility for children**

| Employment status | None | Highest qualification | | | | |
| | | CSE 2-5 | 'O' level | 'A' level | Higher quals. | Degree |
| | | % | % | % | % | % |
| **Men** | | | | | | |
| Employed | 66 | 89 | 91 | 92 | 91 | 86 |
| n (100%) | (243) | (694) | (1437) | (358) | (166) | (844) |
| **Women** | | | | | | |
| Employed | 45 | 73 | 81 | 86 | 86 | 89 |
| full-time | 29 | 56 | 66 | 77 | 78 | 83 |
| part-time | 16 | 17 | 15 | 9 | 8 | 6 |
| n (100%) | (225) | (742) | (1941) | (524) | (203) | (849) |
| **Women without children** | | | | | | |
| Employed | 71 | 94 | 94 | 94 | 94 | 90 |
| full-time | 62 | 87 | 88 | 89 | 88 | 85 |
| part-time | 9 | 7 | 6 | 5 | 6 | 6 |
| At home | 4 | 2 | 1 | <1 | 1 | <1 |
| Other not employed | 25 | 4 | 5 | 6 | 6 | 10 |
| n (100%) | (79) | (414) | (1274) | (428) | (163) | (811) |
| **Women with children** | | | | | | |
| Employed | 30 | 47 | 56 | 51 | 57 | 65 |
| full-time | 10 | 16 | 25 | 25 | 35 | 44 |
| part-time | 19 | 31 | 31 | 26 | 22 | 21 |
| At home | 63 | 50 | 40 | 43 | 35 | 35 |
| Other not employed | 8 | 3 | 5 | 6 | 8 | 0 |
| n (100%) | (145) | (325) | (661) | (96) | (37) | (34) |

At qualification levels below 'A' level, mothers' jobs were more likely to be part-time than full-time. The highly qualified mothers - despite having *younger* children - appeared more closely attached to the full-time labour force than their less well-educated peers. This contrast among mothers was also apparent in the 1958 cohort study, but less so in the 1946 cohort study (Macran et al., 1996).

To summarise, motherhood appeared to lower the chances of full-time employment  more for women who were less qualified. Those with higher qualifications may be presumed to have an advantage in earning power which could help them make child care arrangements. But it seems equally, if not more, likely that the idea of occupation and 'career', involving more continual engagement with the labour market, was also more central to these women's lives.

## Working your way into the labour market

Cohort members who had not left the labour force, for example to look after their families, were relatively sure of being in a job at 26, but what of the years that had gone before? They had lived through the recession of 1991-2. How much unemployment had they encountered?

Table 3.4    Job history to 26 since leaving education: men and women

| Job history | Men | Women | All |
|---|---|---|---|
| | % | % | % |
| Same job since leaving education | 14 | 11 | 12 |
| Others continuously employed | 22 | 23 | 23 |
| Intermittent employment (no spell of unemployment over 4 months) | 29 | 39 | 35 |
| Unemployment: longest spell 4-11 months | 21 | 16 | 18 |
| Unemployment: longest spell 12-23 months | 8 | 6 | 6 |
| Unemployment: longest spell over 2 years, some employment | 5 | 5 | 5 |
| No employment | 1 | 1 | 1 |
| n (100%) | (4028) | (4740) | (8768) |

Without a month-by-month account of their employment record, this question can only be answered impressionistically. A summary of job history once in the labour market was pieced together from answers to various questions on spells in various employment states, and length of time in current job. Short spells of unemployment of three months or less at the beginning of the history were ignored, with a resulting estimate that one third of the cohort had been continuously employed, and that one in seven of the men and one in nine of the women had stayed in their first job. Another third had histories of intermittent employment, mixed with various other experiences, but no more than three months in any one spell of unemployment. Those with the longer periods of unemployment made up the remaining third, along with the one per cent who had never had a job. Men were more likely to report unemployment, and women, intermittent employment.

*Jobs before and at 26*

**Table 3.5   Job history by current employment status at 26**

| Job history | Full-time | Part-time | Unemployed | Education | Sick | At home |
|---|---|---|---|---|---|---|
| | % | % | % | % | % | % |
| **Men** | | | | | | |
| Employed: | | | | | | |
| continuously | 42 | 15 | - | - | - | - |
| intermittently | 31 | 18 | 9 | 53 | 18 | - |
| unemployed | 27 | 67 | 85 | 43 | 61 | - |
| never | - | - | 5 | 4 | 21 | - |
| | | | | | | |
| *n (100%)* | *(3377)* | *(95)* | *(275)* | *(130)* | *(71)* | - |
| **Women** | | | | | | |
| Employed: | | | | | | |
| continuously | 48 | 16 | - | - | - | - |
| intermittently | 35 | 45 | 22 | 66 | 32 | 54 |
| unemployed | 17 | 39 | 72 | 33 | 47 | 42 |
| never | - | - | 6 | 1 | 21 | 43 |
| | | | | | | |
| *n (100%)* | *(3102)* | *(599)* | *(123)* | *(105)* | *(66)* | *(635)* |

**Note**: Unemployed includes 19 cases on training schemes, sick includes temporary and long-term illness.

What were the labour market histories leading up to the snapshot of employment states recorded in 1996? Table 3.5 shows that full-time employees at age 26 were the most likely to have been in continuous employment, and least likely to have had substantial spells of unemployment. Those currently in part-time jobs, especially men, had less complete job records. Two thirds of the men in part-time jobs had had spells of unemployment exceeding four months. Those currently in a job were asked how long they had been there. Nearly one in five appeared to have been with only one employer since starting out, but, at the other end of the spectrum, even more had only been in their current job for short durations - 36 per cent under two years. Hence, within these histories, at one end of the scale there was likely to have been a lot of job changing, and at the other end considerable job stability.

Obviously, those currently unemployed could not have been continuously employed. Most, but not all, had had substantial spells of unemployment (90 per cent of the unemployed men and 78 per cent of the women currently seeking work, including around five per cent who had *never* had a job).

The cohort members' unemployment histories measured in this way are related to their chances of being in full-time employment. As the length of the longest unemployment spell *increased*, the probability of being in a full-time job at 26 *declined*: among men who had been unemployed for as long as two years, less than one in three had a full-time job at the time of the survey, and among women, only one in seven (Table 3.6).

**Table 3.6  Unemployment and subsequent full-time employment**

| Length of longest spell of unemployment | Chances of full-time job at age 26 | |
|---|---|---|
| | %<br>Men | %<br>Women |
| 4-11 months | 81 | 57 |
| 12-23 months | 61 | 35 |
| 2 years or more | 31 | 14 |
| Whole cohort | 85 | 67 |

*Job history and qualifications*

The chances of avoiding prolonged unemployment rose with qualifications. Figure 3.2 shows that three fifths of the group with no qualifications had notched up unemployment lasting over three months, or had never had a job at all. However, it was those with intermediate school leaving qualifications at 'O' and 'A' levels who reported the most continuous employment. Those with 'A' level were most likely to have been in the same job since leaving school. The graduates did not escape unemployment quite as well as those with 'A' levels, probably because many of them entered the labour market in the recession of 1991.

Women tended to have had more work interruption for domestic reasons than men, particularly those with qualifications below 'A' levels (who were also the most likely to have had children). But the main picture of employment continuity and discontinuity was very similar for men and women.

These figures show how vital qualifications were becoming to ensure a reasonably secure location in the labour market. On the other hand, the fact that no more than two fifths of any group had the same job since leaving school, points to the growing instability of modern careers overall.

**Figure 3.2  Job history by highest qualification**

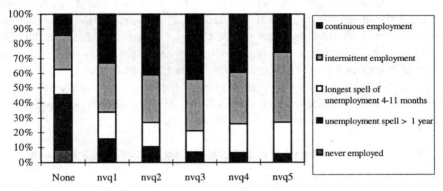

*Further education, training and job history*

Those who had unbroken employment with their current employer might be expected to be on an 'inside track', which would increase their prospects of getting on-the-job training. But there was little difference between them and others who had changed employers while maintaining continuous employment. However, the chances of getting such training fell off substantially with employment discontinuity. Within each type of job history, men were the more likely to have had employer training. The group with the best on-the-job training record were men with continuous employment (40 per cent), while the group with the least such training were women with a spell of unemployment over three months (18 per cent).

Although about a quarter of those in continuous employment had been on a YTS or other Government scheme, the proportion among the unemployed group was much higher (40 per cent). Since experience of YTS would have preceded the period(s) of unemployment, this suggests that far from aiding entry to the labour market, such programmes actually *reduced* the recipients' prospects. The type of schemes attended by the 1970 cohort members may, to some extent at least, account for this.

*Family background and job history*

How well the cohort members fared in their transition to employment was related to their family backgrounds, as assessed by social class at the time of their birth in 1970. Figures 3.3a and 3.3b compare male and female cohort member employment histories for the social classes based (a) on father's occupation and (b) on mother's occupation (if she had one to report).

Both men and women with fathers in social class 1 (Professional) and 2 (Managerial and Technical) had the lowest proportion who had been unemployed for over one year, while those in social class 5 (Unskilled) had the highest. The latter group also had disproportionate numbers who had never been employed. For the children of mothers who were on their own in 1970, there was as great an unemployment risk as if they had been born into a family with a father in an unskilled occupation. Neither type of start in life seemed very auspicious.

**Figure 3.3  Job history by social class of each parent in 1970**

a) **Father's class in 1970**

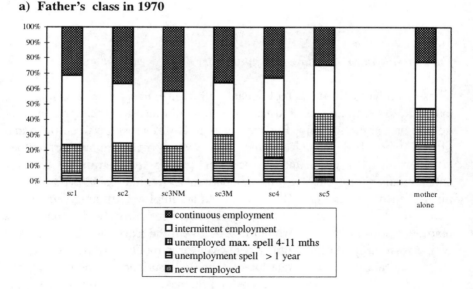

**Figure 3.3 continued**

**b) Mother's class, if employed at time of cohort member's birth**

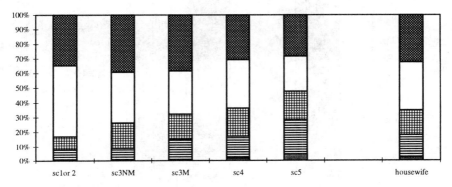

sc1or 2          sc3NM          sc3M          sc4          sc5          housewife

**Note:**  sc = social class; NM = non-manual; M = manual.

## Who gets the good jobs?

*Occupational attainment and the employment structure*

Parents' social class tells us something about their own occupational success. How does this compare with the cohort members' achievement in the labour market? This question can only be answered for those with a job at 26, but this was by far the majority. Figure 3.4 compares the occupational attainments of the men and women in the cohort, grouped together into the same occupational classes as for their parents.

Overall, the distributions for men and women were surprisingly similar. More of the men had reached professional jobs in Social Class 1, but there were more women in the next band of jobs, so that the proportions in Social Classes 1 or 2 were virtually the same. Taken together, the proportions in the combined class 3 were also roughly equivalent, although women were more frequently to be found in the non-manual jobs and men in the skilled manual jobs, reflecting the continuation of the traditional division between men's and women's work.

Notably, a history of unemployment appeared to make a greater difference than gender to the occupation observed in 1996. Those workers with spells of unemployment exceeding a year (seven per cent) were only half as likely as the others to have a job in the top two classes, and were correspondingly over-represented in unskilled work.

**Figure 3.4  Social class of cohort member's job at 26**

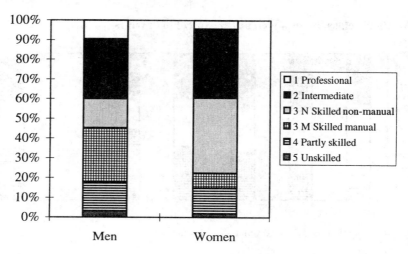

Table 3.7 illustrates how changes in occupational structure had affected these families, and how 26-year-olds' jobs in 1996 compared with those reported by the 1946 cohort at age 26 in 1972. For both sets of men employed in the 1970s - the fathers of our 1970 cohort, and men born in 1946 - over 40 percent of all occupations were in the skilled manual group. Correspondingly, the same proportion of the mothers of the 1970 cohort, and the earlier cohort of women, were classified as non-manual workers, mostly in offices and shops. By 1996, the proportions of men and women in these categories was down - to 28 per cent for men in skilled manual jobs and 38 per cent for women in the skilled non-manual category. The proportion of men doing less skilled work had changed little. For women, however, it had dropped below that of their mothers, and of women aged 26 in 1972.

The upward shift in the structure of opportunities for those in work is seen in the increase in the top two classes, from one fifth of the 1970 cohort's fathers to two fifths of the male cohort members themselves. For women, the comparable figures were 16 per cent of the cohort's mothers and 39 per cent of the female cohort members at age 26.

**Table 3.7    Occupational class distribution across two generations and two cohorts at age 26**

| Social Class (Registrar General's) | Fathers in 1970 | Men aged 26 in 1972 | Sons at 26 in 1996 | Mothers in 1970 | Women aged 26 in 1972 | Daughters at 26 in 1996 |
|---|---|---|---|---|---|---|
| | % | % | % | % | % | % |
| 1 Professional | 6 | 8 | 10 | }16 | 1 | 4 |
| 2 Intermediate | 14 | 19 | 31 | | 23 | 35 |
| 3 Skilled non-manual | 14 | 13 | 15 | 48 | 45 | 38 |
| 3 Skilled manual | 47 | 42 | 28 | 7 | 7 | 8 |
| 4 Partly skilled | 14 | 14 | 14 | 28 | 18 | 13 |
| 5 Unskilled | 5 | 3 | 3 | 1 | 5 | 2 |
| n (100%) | (7690) | (1438) | (3211) | (5056) | (720) | (3881) |

Note: Data for the 1946 cohort courtesy of the MRC National Survey  for Health and Development.  Taken from Joshi and Newell (1989), weighted sample of employees with known pay.

*Occupation and qualifications*

As we have seen, the route to high level occupations is much surer for those with qualifications. Eight out of ten graduates had a job in the Professional or Intermediate Classes (1 & 2), as did approaching three fifths of those with other higher qualifications, half with 'A' level, one third with 'O' level, one fifth CSE and down to one tenth of those with no qualifications. Higher qualifications were not, however, essential: 30 per cent of the 'top two' types of job - mostly at the intermediate level - were held by people whose highest qualification was the equivalent of 'O' level.

*Parents' occupation*

Qualifications mediate the effects of family background on occupational attainment. As we saw in the last chapter, fathers' social class was strongly related to the level of qualification the cohort members had reached. We might expect, therefore, to find a similarly strong relationship between fathers' occupational attainment and that of their children.

Figures 3.5a and 3.5b analyse the cohort members' jobs against those of their parents. For both males and females, there was an association between class of origin and class of employed cohort members at 26, although there was a stronger trend towards social mobility. Overall, these 26-year-olds were further up the occupational ladder than their parents had been at the time of their birth. The pattern for men and women was similar if the distinction between the manual and non-manual types of Class 3 jobs is ignored.

Figures 3.5a and 3.5b provide evidence of the social mobility of the cohort members, that is, the extent to which they had moved up or down the occupational scale compared with their parents. We would expect general movement upwards because of the overall changes in the labour market between 1970 and 1996. The overall evidence of social mobility is summarised in table 3.8.

**Figure 3.5  Cohort member's social class of occupation in 1996, by father's social class in 1970**

### a) Men

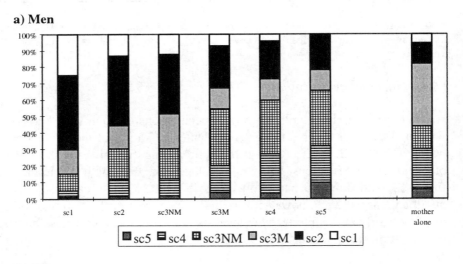

### b) Women

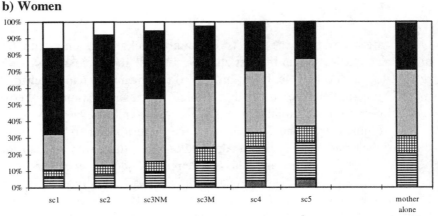

**Note:** sc = social class; NM =non-manual; M = manual.

**Table 3.8    Class mobility between father's and cohort member's occupation: employed cohort member**

| Social classes | Men | | | Women | | |
|---|---|---|---|---|---|---|
| | same | up | down | same | up | down |
| Uncondensed | 30% | 44% | 25% | 20% | 57% | 23% |
| Condensed | 44% | 36% | 20% | 45% | 37% | 18% |
| | *(n = 2754)* | | | *(n = 3104)* | | |

**Note:** The row of figures labelled 'uncondensed' shows the percentage mobility across all six social classes; the row labelled 'condensed' shows the percentage mobility when sc1 and sc2 are combined and sc3NM and sc3M are combined.

If we count all crossing of social class 'boundaries' as social mobility, we see that only 30 per cent of the men and 20 per cent of the women stayed in the same occupational class as their fathers, and that most moves appeared to be upward. However, it is doubtful whether the divide between skilled manual and non-manual jobs necessarily constitutes a division between jobs of unequal prestige or earning power. Hence in the second row of Table 3.8, Class 3 (manual and non-manual) is treated as a single class. The intermediate (technical and managerial) and professional classes (Social Classes 1 and 2) are also combined, since, at age 26, many of the intermediates may be on their way to more senior positions, and we are comparing them with fathers, many of whom were older than 26 in 1970. With this simplification of the mobility table, the patterns for men and women converged. In the order of 45 per cent were in the same class as their fathers; just over one third had experienced upward mobility, while around one in five had moved 'down'.

## Who gets the high pay?

Was the social status of the range of jobs the 26-year-olds held reflected in what they got paid for doing them? For most of the cohort members in employment, there was usable information about their take-home pay - earnings after deductions of tax and pension contributions. The mid-point of the range of pay packets was £180 per week: £203 for the men and £158 for the women (Table 3.9). Female employees thus took home, on average, 24 per cent less than their male counterparts. Actually, the lowest paid women had half the pay of the lowest paid men, because most often they were part-timers. Men also work longer hours than women, especially when they have children.

Women's earnings fell below men's, on average, but, as Table 3.9 shows, particularly at the bottom end of the pay range. There was a gap of nine per cent in the average hourly pay of women and men, but this gap has been closing over the last 24 years: it was 37 per cent in 1972 for the 26-year-olds in the 1946 cohort, and 29 per cent in 1991 for the 33-year-olds in the 1958 cohort. Despite all the problems of comparing our 26-year-olds with the 33-year-olds, the evidence points to continuing progress towards gender equality in pay as well as employment patterns.

**Table 3.9    Net weekly earnings (£s) of employees at 26 at three points on the distribution**

|  | Average in bottom tenth | Half earn less than | Average in top tenth |
|---|---|---|---|
| Men | 114.11 | 203.16 | 440.75 |
| Women | 56.15 | 157.67 | 348.76 |
| All | 72.55 | 180.36 | 402.44 |

Where is the highest pay to be found and which groups command it? Table 3.10 compares the average pay per hour (net of taxes) for different occupations and between groups of cohort members with different social and educational backgrounds. The findings reinforce our picture of the factors that increase the chances of occupational success. Hourly pay increased with educational attainment and with father's social class at birth. There appeared to be no systematic differences in mean wages across different family types, except that having had a child by age 26 appeared to reduce hourly pay. Another surprising contrast with workers of all ages, and with the earlier cohort studies, was that the hourly pay of part-time workers was not much different from that of full-timers. This may be because full-timers aged 26 were relatively poorly paid in comparison with older workers, or because 26-year-old part-timers were better paid than other part-timers.

**Table 3.10 Mean net hourly earnings for selected groups of employees**

| Average pay | Men £ | Men n | Women £ | Women n | All £ | All n |
|---|---|---|---|---|---|---|
| | 5.37 | 2736 | 4.91 | 3225 | 5.12 | 5961 |
| **By social class of occupation** | | | | | | |
| Professional | 6.30 | 255 | 6.90 | 138 | 6.51 | 393 |
| Managerial/technical | 6.02 | 809 | 5.55 | 1081 | 5.75 | 1890 |
| Skilled non-manual | 5.26 | 395 | 4.60 | 1172 | 4.77 | 1567 |
| Skilled manual | 4.77 | 607 | 4.13 | 200 | 4.61 | 807 |
| Partly skilled | 4.40 | 345 | 3.80 | 366 | 4.09 | 711 |
| Unskilled | 3.94 | 57 | 3.26 | 55 | 3.61 | 112 |
| **By highest qualification** | | | | | | |
| Degree | 6.22 | 639 | 5.92 | 667 | 6.06 | 1306 |
| Diploma | 5.53 | 122 | 5.09 | 153 | 5.29 | 275 |
| 'A'-level | 5.83 | 287 | 5.37 | 400 | 5.56 | 687 |
| 'O'-level | 5.24 | 998 | 4.51 | 1358 | 4.82 | 2356 |
| CSE 2-5 | 4.70 | 456 | 4.39 | 443 | 4.55 | 899 |
| None | 4.04 | 101 | 3.73 | 82 | 3.90 | 183 |
| **By father's social class** | | | | | | |
| Professional | 6.25 | 168 | 6.05 | 175 | 6.15 | 343 |
| Managerial/technical | 5.94 | 311 | 5.10 | 399 | 5.47 | 710 |
| Skilled non-manual | 5.81 | 384 | 5.39 | 433 | 5.59 | 817 |
| Skilled manual | 5.19 | 1065 | 4.76 | 1349 | 4.95 | 2414 |
| Partly skilled | 4.76 | 323 | 4.58 | 340 | 4.67 | 663 |
| Unskilled | 4.27 | 91 | 4.00 | 104 | 4.13 | 195 |
| Others | 5.59 | 76 | 4.39 | 89 | 4.93 | 165 |
| Unsupported mother | 5.04 | 63 | 4.45 | 81 | 4.71 | 144 |

The relationships between pay and the background variables shown in Table 3.10 was analysed further by means of multiple regression analysis. This statistical technique allows us to examine the effects of a number of background variables in turn on an outcome variable such as income, holding constant the effects of all the other background variables. The results suggest that education increases wages. Other things being equal, those with 'O' levels were paid around seven per cent more than those with lower or no qualifications. The payoff rose to 25 per cent for a University degree. The returns on education appeared slightly higher for women than for men, ranging from eight per cent for 'O' levels to 30 per cent for a degree for women, as opposed to seven per cent to 22 per cent for men. Similar effects were found for the 1958 cohort (Paci and Joshi, 1996).

The regression analysis also identified an additional positive effect on wages of the father's social class, independent of the cohort member's own qualifications and other factors. Being born to a father in a professional job in 1970 went with a 13 per cent mark-up on wages.

Finally, the regression analysis allowed us to explore the effect of training on wages. The results were striking. Work-related training appeared to increase pay by over 12 per cent and 11 per cent respectively for men and women. Having done a course leading to qualifications had a small positive effect on men's pay but not on women's, while having been on Youth Training Schemes appeared to have *reduced* pay by as much as six per cent for men and eight per cent for women. This is in line with other shorter-term studies questioning the value of YTS in the 1980s to participants' pay prospects. While investigation of other relevant factors such as work experience, region and health would be needed for a complete assessment, it is clear that going on YTS cannot be identified with the success stories in the 1990s labour market.

### Who makes it to the top and who falls back?

The previous section pointed to the degree of social mobility in the 1970 cohort. Less than half the cohort members stayed in the same occupational class as their fathers, though we have to acknowledge that part of this movement was due to the general occupational up-grading that was taking place in the economy, as unskilled and partly skilled work declined. We also saw evidence of a narrowing of the gap between men's and women's pay and prospects in the labour market. Finally, we bring together these different elements of achievement, examining in more detail the extent to which the more individualised careers of the 1970 cohort were paying off in terms of upwards occupational mobility.

Figure 3.6 refines the measure of successful entry into the labour market, focusing on those cohort members who had qualifications at least to 'A' level (NVQ3) standard and who had no substantial spells of unemployment. These criteria accounted for about a quarter of all cases. As the graph shows, the chances of meeting these criteria varied widely by social origins. There was about a tenfold difference between the success rates of the most advantaged cohort members (with fathers in Social Class 1) and those from the least advantaged origins (lone mothers for boys and fathers in social class 5 for girls). This suggests that the old structures by which pathways to occupational achievement were established in the past are still quite firmly in place. Those at the bottom of the ladder tend to stay there. On the other hand, the fact that there was surprisingly little to differentiate the young men from the young women suggests that at least the structural constraints associated with gender may be breaking down. As was concluded in the last chapter, the equal opportunities policies of the 1980s appear to be paying off.

**Figure 3.6  Labour market high flyers by social origin: no spell of unemployment over 3 months and qualified to 'A' levels or above**

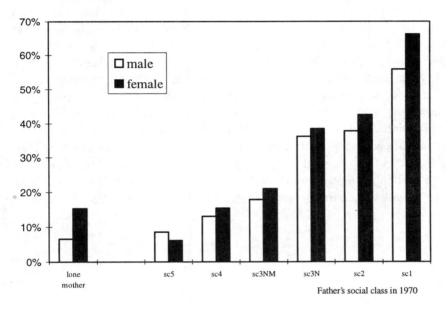

**Careers for almost everyone?**

The launch of the 1970 cohort on to the labour market of the 1990s appeared, on the whole, to have been a success, with full-time jobs in knowledge-based occupations for the majority - women as well as men. We found striking differences between cohort members, depending on their attachment to paid work. We also found that class background still continued to exercise an effect on occupational outcomes.

Gender differences were not as big as might have been expected, given the experience of previous generations. Improved education and training opportunities, coupled with the equal opportunities imperatives which took root in the 1980s, appear to have benefited young women particularly. The gap in occupational position and pay is less than it was for their predecessors. Parenthood, however, still affects the occupational patterns of women more than men, because of their exit from the labour market, or entry into part-time employment, during the period of having and bringing up children. Whether the employment prospects for the women in the 1970 cohort will begin to diverge from those of the men, as more of them become parents, remains to be seen.

The answer to the question of who gets the good jobs is clear, however. As in the past, the well-educated sons and daughters of socially advantaged parents were the most likely to thrive in the labour market of 1996. They enjoyed, on average, greater employment security, better career prospects, higher occupational status and more pay than the others. The picture was rather different for many of the poorly educated with a disadvantaged family background. Compared with their parents, the problems of this group appeared to be accentuated with the upgrading of occupations, and the higher premium placed by employers on educational qualifications. While being born female thus appears to be less of an obstacle to equal employment opportunities amongst this generation, at least for the child-free, upwardly mobile contingent of 26-year-olds, being born into a particular family background continues to make a dramatic difference to the chances of an individual 'getting on, getting by or getting nowhere'.

# 4 Where You Live and Who You Live With

ELSA FERRI and KATE SMITH

## Introduction

The transformations which took place in the domains of education, training and the labour market during the years in which the 1970 birth cohort progressed to adulthood, were matched by equally dramatic changes in the world of personal relationships and family life. The growing significance of negotiated, rather than ascribed, personal relationships; multiple options - or, at least, decisions - concerning where, and with whom, one lives, all contribute to a range of alternatives to the traditional sequence of moving from the parental home to married life, and thence to parenthood. These alternatives are reflected in the most important demographic trends relating to partnership and family formation which have taken place over the lifetime of the 1970 cohort. The most salient of these for a group now in their 20s include the marked decline in marriage rates and the continued rise in cohabitation. In the area of reproduction, first births are occurring much later, and, increasingly, outside the context of marriage.

However, the influence of social and economic changes, in particular those producing the polarisation which has taken place in many aspects of British society in recent years, means that different groups will have had contrasting experiences with regard to their relationships and living arrangements. For some, prolonged education and training, and energies invested in career development are likely to be linked to delay in 'settling down' with a partner, and in starting a family. At the other end of the spectrum, for those who have not obtained high qualifications and marketable skills, the insecurity of the 'flexible' labour market, and the reduced access to both owner occupation and local authority housing which took place from the late 1980s, will no doubt have inhibited their moves to independent living.

This chapter looks at the situation at age 26 of the 1970 cohort in the areas of relationships and living arrangements. Where, and with whom, were the cohort members living in 1996? How many were still in their parental home, and how many had set up their own household with a partner, either in marriage or cohabitation? How many had become parents, and in what kind of families were they raising their children? Most importantly, what characterised those who had arrived at these very different locations by the time they had reached their mid-twenties?

## Partnerships

### *Marriage*

Much concern is expressed nowadays, by different political parties, religious bodies and sections of the media, at the growing unpopularity and fragility of marriage in British society. Marriage rates have reached their lowest level since records began around 150 years ago, while Britain currently has the highest divorce rate in Europe, with four new marriages in ten breaking down (Utting, 1995). There is a widespread view that marriage as an institution needs to be strengthened and supported: one recent commentary proposed the drafting of individual time-limited marriage contracts for those without children; an example, perhaps, of the ways in which attempts are being made to reformulate social institutions within the context of an individualistic culture (Wilkinson, 1997).

A less alarmist perspective suggests that marriage would be 'going out of fashion' only if cohabiting couples explicitly rejected it, or if divorcees were determined not to remarry, both of which are far from being the case (Utting, 1995). What is certainly true is that the median age at marriage has risen markedly; in the case of men from 23 in 1971 to 28 in 1993, and for women from 21 to 26 over the same period (*Social Trends 1996*). Indeed, it has been pointed out that, over the past 30 years, the median age at first marriage for both men and women has risen from its lowest to its highest recorded levels (OPCS,1994).

The 1970 cohort will thus have been born to parents who were particularly likely to have married young, but will themselves be influenced by the recent trend towards later marriage. Our survey findings showed that just one in three of the 26-year-old women, and less than a quarter of the men, were currently married and living with their spouse (Figure 4.1). A very small number of these couples (just 32 women and 14 men) were already involved in second marriages.

The most common age at marriage was 25 for both men and women, although considerably more women than men had married at younger ages. Very few - just one per cent of the men and four per cent of the women in the cohort - had married in their teens.

Most of these married couples - nearly three quarters of the men and two thirds of the women - had lived together prior to marrying. This fits in with current demographic trends indicating that pre-marital cohabitation has become a majority practice within the space of a generation (*Social Trends 1996*). Other recent statistics, however, also show higher breakdown rates among marriages preceded by cohabitation (Haskey, 1992).

Almost all of the married couples in the 1970 cohort had established independent households of their own by the time of the survey. Just three per cent of the men concerned, and two per cent of the women, were living with their parents or in-laws.

**Figure 4.1   Per cent of cohort members living in different domestic arrangements at 26**

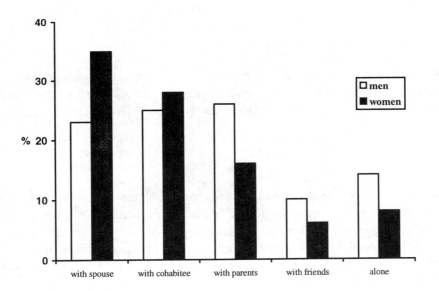

*Cohabitation*

The decline in marriage rates already referred to has been accompanied by a marked increase in cohabitation. At the time when the *parents* of most of the 1970 cohort married - in the late 1960s - only six per cent of women lived with their future husbands before marriage. By the early 1990s, this figure had risen 10-fold (Kiernan and Estaugh, 1993), and cohabitation at some stage had become a majority experience of both women and men in the 25-29 age group (Buck et al., 1994).

About a quarter of both the men and the women in the 1970 cohort were cohabiting at age 26 (Figure 4.1). In all but a few of these relationships, the cohort member concerned was single; the remaining cases had already experienced a broken marriage, and were either separated or divorced.

Three quarters of the men, and two thirds of the women, in cohabiting relationships had been living with their partners for three years or less. Recent research in this area has found that such relationships rarely last longer than five years, proceeding either to marriage or separation (Kiernan and Estaugh,1993). There is evidence, too, that breaking up is much more common among the cohabiting than among the married (Buck et al., 1994). We will have to await future follow-ups of this cohort to discover what happens to the relationships recorded in the 1996 survey - including whether cohabitation proves to be a long-term, or permanent, alternative to marriage as well as, hitherto, a precursor.

## The unpartnered

While a considerable proportion of the cohort were married or cohabiting by age 26, just over half of the men, and nearly four out of ten of the women, were not living with a partner. About half of these cohort members, however, reported that they were currently 'in a relationship'.

### Living with parents

The most common situation among the unpartnered 26-year-olds was to be living with their parents - as many as 26 per cent of the men, and 16 per cent of the women (Figure 4.1). Almost all of this group were single, although it also included the small group of married couples already mentioned. There were, too, some cohort members who appeared to have returned to their parents' home following separation or divorce.

There has been a trend in recent years for a growing number of young adults, especially males, to remain - or return to - living in their parental home. Those cohort members living with their parents at 26 were by no means a homogeneous group, however. At one end of the spectrum, the trend reflects the marked growth in the numbers entering higher education and thus delaying their entry to the labour market and the achievement of financial independence. In contrast, other research in this area has observed that social and economic conditions in the 1990s have made it increasingly difficult for young people to make the transition to independent living. These include the problems of achieving an adequate and secure income from employment, the lack of affordable housing and the reduction, for a variety of reasons, of support from their families which would assist them to become independent (Jones, 1995). Also of significance here was the withdrawal of Housing Benefit in 1988 to young people under 25, representing an implicit shift in social policy regarding the length of parents' financial obligations towards their children.

*Living independently*

The social changes outlined in Chapter 1 are also mirrored in the growth of the 'independent lifestyle'. With the widespread extension of the time spent in education, and the pursuit of career and personal development, an interim period between leaving the parental home and forming a new family has for many become a new rite of passage. However, as Jones (1995) has pointed out, this independent lifestyle is heavily dependent on access to an adequate income and appropriate housing.

Among the 1970 cohort members who were living independently, there was a higher proportion of young men living on their own (14 per cent compared with eight per cent of the women), and a similar difference in the numbers who were sharing accommodation, mostly with friends - or in a few cases, siblings - (10 per cent and six per cent respectively) (Figure 4.1). This gender difference no doubt reflects the fact that more women than men were married or cohabiting by age 26. However, other recent research has noted a particular propensity for young, never-married men to live alone, and has linked this also to greater geographical mobility in pursuit of advancement in the labour market (Hall et al., 1997).

As with the group living with their parents, all but a handful of those living alone or sharing with friends were single; just a small proportion had experienced broken marriages.

*Divorced/separated*

Altogether, two per cent of men and five per cent of women in the 1970 cohort had experienced marital breakdown by the age of 26. About half of the divorced group had acquired new partners by the time of the survey, but the separated, especially men, were more likely to be living on their own.

The 1970 cohort was born at the time of the implementation of the 1969 Divorce Reform Act. The marked, and continuing, rise in divorce which followed meant that the break-up of their parents' marriage would have been an increasingly common experience for this cohort during their childhood. Future analysis will indicate what, if any, relationship exists between the stability of the families in which they grew up and that of their own adult relationships. It is interesting to note at this stage, however, that research based on the cohorts born in 1958 and 1946 has found that the divorce of their parents was one of the key factors accounting for marital breakdown among the subjects of these studies

(Kiernan, 1997).

## Parenthood

As noted at the beginning of this chapter, the changing patterns of adult relationships in our society are matched by striking trends in the timing of the transition to parenthood, and in the context of family life. The steady rise in the age of mothers at first birth over recent years means that, at the time of the 1996 survey, the 1970 cohort were, at 26, below the current average age (28.3) at which women have their first child (OPCS, 1996). The diverse settings in which child-rearing currently takes place are exemplified by such facts as that about one in three births today occur outside marriage; one in five families with dependent children are headed by a lone parent; and high rates of repartnership following divorce or separation mean that one in 12 dependent children now live in stepfamilies (Utting, 1995).

A fifth of the men and a third of the women in the 1970 cohort had had at least one child born to them by the age of 26. Most of those who had become parents had only one child, but a small minority (four per cent of women and just one per cent of men) had three or more.

The great majority of the fathers and mothers concerned (95 per cent and 77 per cent respectively) were bringing up their children in a two-parent household, and most were married rather than cohabiting (Figure 4.2). Thus although, overall, cohort members with partners were almost as likely to be cohabiting as married, *parenthood* was much more strongly associated with marriage. For most of these 26-year-old parents, therefore, the conventional nuclear family remained the most typical setting in which they were raising their children, a finding which, in line with studies of the 1958 cohort at age 33, puts in some perspective the alarmist claims concerning the demise of the traditional family (Ferri and Smith, 1996).

However, other information about the living arrangements of these parents also revealed many of the complexities of family life in 1990s Britain. As many as a quarter of the fathers were not living with all or some of their children. This points, perhaps, to a particular instability associated with *young* fatherhood: the corresponding figure among fathers in the 1958 cohort at age 33 was approximately one seventh (Ferri, 1993). Conversely, almost one in five of the 26-year-old mothers were lone parents at the time of the survey, similar to the proportion of 33-year-old mothers in the 1958 cohort who had experienced lone parenthood at some stage (Ferri, 1993).

**Figure 4.2    Per cent of cohort members with children in different family situations**

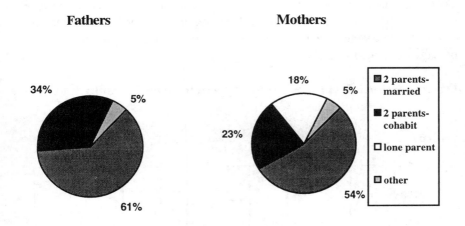

For both sexes, one in five had a current partner who was not the other natural parent of their children. Three per cent of men, but less than one per cent of women, had stepchildren living in their household, while three per cent of men also, and no fewer than ten per cent of women, had current partners whose own child(ren) lived elsewhere. All of these figures reflect the continuing high probability that children will remain with their mother when their parents separate or, in some cases, never set up home together.

**Characteristics of different groups**

So far, we have indicated the great diversity of locations at which the 1970 cohort members had arrived by the age of 26, in terms of where, and with whom, they were living. About two thirds of the women, and nearly half the men, were living in independent households with a spouse or partner, and a substantial minority had become parents. The remainder were more or less equally divided between those living independent lives alone, or with friends, and those remaining in, or returned to, their parental home.

How similar or different were these various groups in terms of their previous experiences and characteristics, and other aspects of their contemporary lives such as their employment situation, status of current occupation, and the kind of homes they had acquired?

*Married couples*

Cohort members who were married at 26 differed markedly from their peers who remained single, both in their current lives and in their earlier experiences. For example, they were much less likely to have had fathers in professional or managerial occupations (Figure 4.3).

**Figure 4.3   Social class at birth by current partnership and living arrangements**

### a) Men

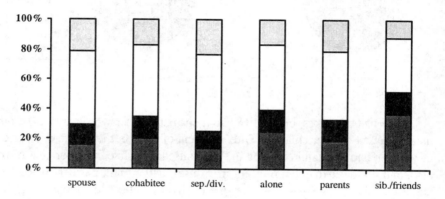

### b) Women

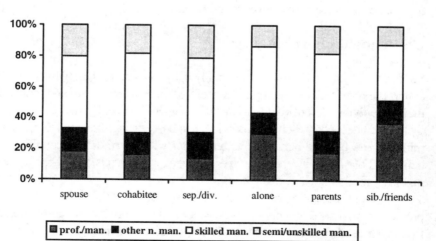

■ prof./man.   ■ other n. man.   □ skilled man.   □ semi/unskilled man.

Given the strong relationship between social origins and educational achievement (see Chapter 2), it was not surprising to find that they were also less likely to have gained high educational qualifications - only 11 per cent of the married men and 12 per cent of the married women had a degree or equivalent, compared with about four out of ten of those living alone or with friends (Figure 4.4).

**Figure 4.4   Highest qualification by current partnership and living arrangements**

**a) Men**

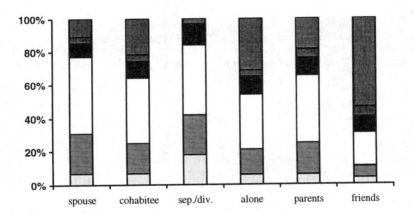

**b) Women**

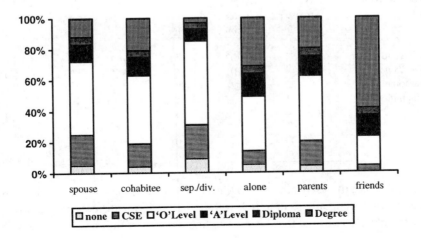

However, although they did not have the advantages of higher qualifications, married men were more firmly established in the labour market at 26 than those in any other group, with 93 per cent  in full time employment (Table 4.1). Young married women, on the other hand, were much less likely to be in full-time employment (57 per cent) than their single counterparts (81 per cent). More of the married women were either working part-time or at home full-time, which was, as we shall see, linked to motherhood.

**Table 4.1   Current employment status by partnership and living arrangements at 26**

### a) Men

| Employment status | With spouse % | With partner % | Sep./ divorced % | Alone % | With parents % | With friends % |
|---|---|---|---|---|---|---|
| Works full-time | 93 | 88 | 81 | 77 | 81 | 76 |
| Works part-time | 2 | 2 | - | 2 | 2 | 5 |
| At home | <1 | <1 | 2 | <1 | - | - |
| Unemployed | 3 | 6 | 10 | 9 | 10 | 5 |
| Other | 2 | 4 | 8 | 11 | 7 | 15 |
| | | | | | | |
| Total | 100 | 100 | 100 | 100 | 100 | 100 |
| n (100%) | (891) | (900) | (82) | (498) | (993) | (402) |

### b) Women

| Employment status | With spouse % | With partner % | Sep./ divorced % | Alone % | With parents % | With friends % |
|---|---|---|---|---|---|---|
| Works full-time | 57 | 70 | 50 | 81 | 82 | 81 |
| Works part-time | 19 | 10 | 16 | 4 | 7 | 3 |
| At home | 20 | 12 | 29 | - | - | - |
| Unemployed | 1 | 3 | 1 | 5 | 3 | 3 |
| Other | 4 | 5 | 4 | 10 | 9 | 13 |
| | | | | | | |
| Total | 100 | 100 | 100 | 100 | 100 | 100 |
| n (100%) | (1615) | (1119) | (225) | (323) | (750) | (312) |

Among the married,  over a third of those working were in professional or managerial occupations, slightly less than the figure for the cohort as a whole, and considerably less than that for those living alone or with friends (Figure 4.5).

**Figure 4.5  Social class at 26 by current partnership and living arrangements**

**a) Men**

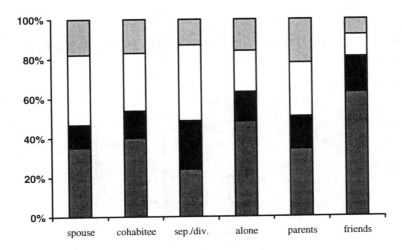

**b) Women**

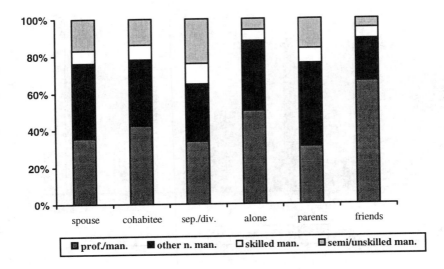

Marriage, and high levels of male full-time employment were, not surprisingly, also associated with relatively early establishment in the housing market. Three quarters of both men and women in the married group were living in owner occupied accommodation, compared with less than half of the entire cohort (Figure 4.6).

**Figure 4.6   Current tenure by partnership and living arrangements at 26**
**a) Men**

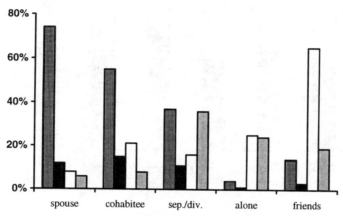

**b) Women**

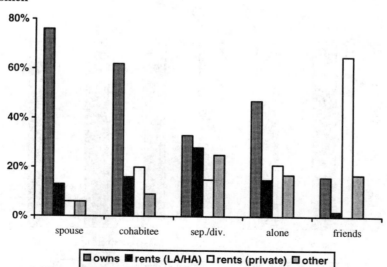

*Marriage and parenthood*  Just under half of both men and women who were married at 26 had also made the transition to parenthood. Further analyses revealed a number of ways in which those who had already become parents differed from those who were still childless.

As far as their own families of origin were concerned, those with children at 26 came from less advantaged social backgrounds than those without: only half as many had  fathers in professional or managerial jobs. There were even more marked differences in the qualifications the two groups had achieved, with parenthood strongly associated with lower achievement. This was especially marked amongst women: childless married women were ten times more likely than mothers to have gained a degree or equivalent (Figure 4.7).

**Figure  4.7  Highest educational qualification for different parent groups at 26**

**a) Men**

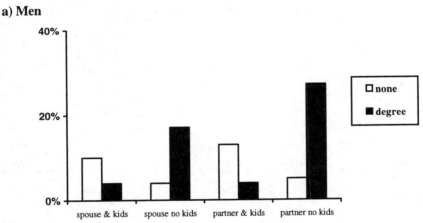

**b) Women**

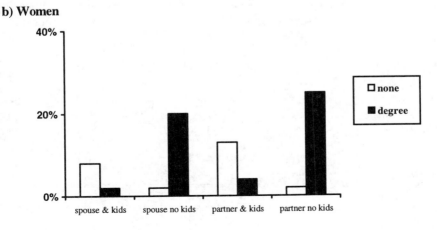

As far as their current employment situation was concerned, there was little difference between the fathers and the childless married men in the proportions in full-time employment (over 90 per cent in each case), although there were more than twice as many fathers as childless in the small group who were unemployed (Table 4.2). The main difference among the married men was in the status of their occupations: more than two fifths of those without children worked in the professional/managerial sector compared to just over a quarter of the fathers (Figure 4.8a).

**Table 4.2    Current employment status for different parental groups at 26**

**a) Men**

| Employment status | Spouse & kids | Spouse no kids | Partner & kids | Partner no kids | Lone parent |
|---|---|---|---|---|---|
| | % | % | % | % | % |
| Works full-time | 91 | 94 | 79 | 91 | 80 |
| Works part-time | 1 | 2 | 2 | 2 | - |
| At home | <1 | <1 | 2 | - | 20 |
| Unemployed | 4 | 2 | 15 | 3 | - |
| Other | 3 | 2 | 2 | 4 | - |
| | | | | | |
| Total | 100 | 100 | 100 | 100 | 100 |
| n (100%) | (416) | (475) | (234) | (691) | (5) |

**b) Women**

| Employment status | Spouse & kids | Spouse no kids | Partner & kids | Partner no kids | Lone parent |
|---|---|---|---|---|---|
| | % | % | % | % | % |
| Works full-time | 21 | 88 | 23 | 86 | 15 |
| Works part-time | 33 | 7 | 26 | 6 | 21 |
| At home | 41 | 1 | 45 | 1 | 58 |
| Unemployed | 2 | 1 | 2 | 3 | 2 |
| Other | 4 | 3 | 5 | 5 | 4 |
| | | | | | |
| Total | 100 | 100 | 100 | 100 | 100 |
| n (100%) | (761) | (854) | (328) | (882) | (238) |

Predictably, there was a striking difference in the employment rate of mothers and childless married women, with four times as many of the childless working full-time. However, a considerable proportion (over 50 per cent) of the young mothers were in the labour market, although most were in part-time jobs. There were also marked variations in the occupational status of the two groups, with nearly as twice as many of the childless in professional or managerial jobs, and nearly three times as many of the mothers in partly skilled or unskilled work.

Whether or not mothers are in the labour market is dictated by economic considerations as well as personal choice or fulfilment. Recent research based on the 1958 cohort has noted that families with young children very often need two good incomes to achieve economic security and adequate living standards (Ferri and Smith, 1996). Our findings suggest that the relatively poor qualifications and low status occupations of the majority of these young parents could make this an uphill struggle.

**Figure 4.8   Social class at 26 for different parent groups**

**a) Men**

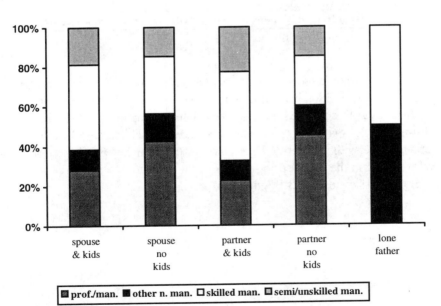

**Figure 4.8 continued**

**b) Women**

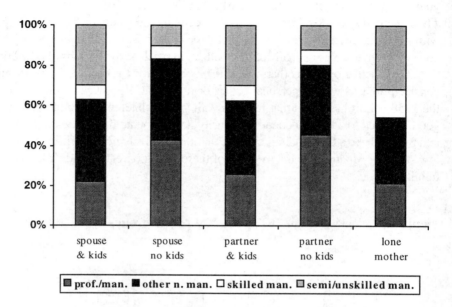

A further contrast between parents and childless couples emerged with respect to their position in the housing market. We have already seen that married couples overall contained by far the highest proportion of home owners. However, this was much more common among the childless (83 per cent) than among those with children (67 per cent). A much higher proportion of parents were renting in the social sector - 23 per cent compared to just three per cent of their childless counterparts (Figure 4.9).

**Figure 4.9  Current tenure for different parent groups at 26**

a) Men

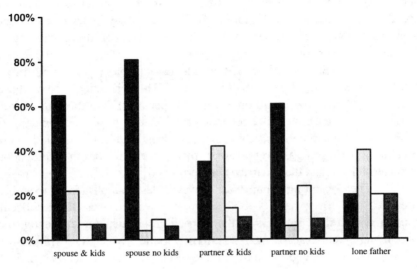

b) Women

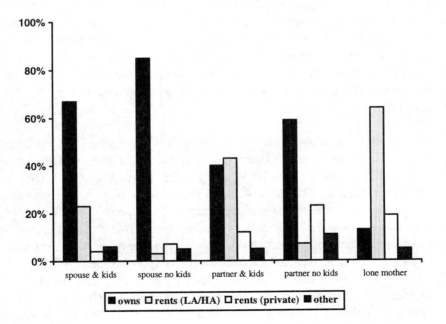

*Cohabiting couples*

Cohort members in cohabiting relationships at the time of the survey came from very similar backgrounds to those who were married, in terms of their fathers' social class of occupation (Figure 4.3). However, they differed with regard to their educational achievement, with twice as many of the cohabiting group having a degree or equivalent (Figure 4.4).

Like their married peers, the vast majority of the cohabiting men were employed full-time (88 per cent) (Table 4.1). The cohabiting women, however, were more likely to be in full-time work (70 per cent) than those in the married group (57 per cent), no doubt reflecting the fact that fewer had children. Given their superior qualifications, it was not surprising that both men and women in cohabiting relationships were rather more likely to be in professional or managerial jobs than their married counterparts (Figure 4.5).

The cohabiting group was, however, less established in their housing situation. Just over half of both men and women were owner occupiers, compared with three quarters of the married group, while a substantial number were living in rented accommodation, mostly in the private sector (Figure 4.6).

These findings would seem to suggest that education and career development had been a more significant feature of the early adult lives of those who, by age 26, had committed themselves to cohabitation rather than marriage, and who had not, or not yet, embarked upon the ladder of home ownership. Utting (1995) notes that establishing oneself in the labour market may take precedence over formalising a relationship by marriage. But economic uncertainty, especially job insecurity, may also deter this: McRae (1993) found that many cohabiting couples with children were put off marrying by the costs of a wedding.

*Cohabitation and parenthood*  About a quarter of those who were cohabiting at 26 had also become parents. There were even more differences between them and their childless counterparts than among the married couples. Far fewer cohabiting fathers and mothers had fathers in professional or managerial occupations than was the case among their childless peers. There were striking differences, too, in the qualifications obtained by the two groups. For both men and women, the proportions who had obtained a degree or equivalent was six times greater among the childless than among the parents (Figure 4.7).

Whereas there was little difference between the employment levels of married men according to whether or not they had children, this was not so among the cohabiting. No less than one in seven of the cohabiting fathers were unemployed - far higher than the figure for childless cohabiting men or married fathers (Table 4.2). Furthermore, amongst those who were working, only half as many cohabiting fathers as those without children worked in the professional/ managerial sectors (Figure 4.8).

As with the married women, far fewer cohabiting mothers than their childless counterparts worked full-time (23 per cent as against 86 per cent), while almost half were at home full-time. Similarly, too, employed cohabiting mothers were more than twice as likely as the childless to be working in unskilled or partly skilled manual jobs.

The contrast between the parents and the childless was also evident with regard to the families' housing circumstances. While six out of ten of the childless cohabitees were home owners, the figure for parents was only about a third (Figure 4.9). Those with children were, by contrast, even more likely than their married counterparts to be renting in the social sector (43 per cent compared to seven per cent of the childless).

*Divorced/separated*

The small group of cohort members who had already experienced separation or divorce by the age of 26 were also those who had married at a particularly early age. Research using data from the 1946 and 1958 cohorts has established a clear link between youthful marriage and subsequent divorce (Kiernan, 1997). Our survey findings also showed that while the separated and divorced were only slightly more likely than those currently married to have had fathers in manual occupations, this group contained by far the highest proportion with low educational achievement. This was particularly marked amongst the men, with those who had experienced marital breakdown nearly three times more likely than the married to have no formal qualifications (Figure 4.4). Among the women, twice as many in the separated or divorced group were without qualifications. It is also important, however, to report Kiernan's finding that the link between low achievement and divorce in the 1946 and 1958 cohort studies was largely accounted for by age at marriage.

Not surprisingly in view of their lack of qualifications, the divorced/separated group were also experiencing less favourable circumstances at age 26. The men in this group reported the highest level of unemployment at the time of the survey - 10 per cent, which was more than three times greater than the figure for the married men (Table 4.1). The divorced/separated men who were in work were much less likely than the married to be in professional/ managerial jobs (Figure 4.5).

Labour market participation was also lower among the separated or divorced women (65 per cent) than any other group (Table 4.1). In addition, those who were in employment were rather less likely to work full-time than their married counterparts. More were at home, which is unsurprising as this group was the most likely to have children. Those who were working were notable for their poor labour market position, with a quarter in semi or unskilled manual jobs (Figure 4.5).

Relatively few separated or divorced cohort members owned their own home (about one in three compared to three quarters of those currently married) (Figure 4.6). While a substantial minority (about one in five men) had returned to their parental home, more of the divorced/separated women were renting in the public/social sector than was the case in any other group.

We do not know at this stage the nature of the links between the circumstances and experiences characterising the cohort members who had experienced marital breakdown; for example, whether poor qualifications and labour market opportunities had attracted them to early marriage, or whether early marriage (and in some cases parenthood) had been an obstacle to the pursuit of education, training and career development; whether their vulnerability in the labour and housing market, and, perhaps, early parenthood, had put pressure on their relationships, or whether marital breakdown itself had had an adverse impact on their working lives and living arrangements.

*Lone parents*

Virtually all of the cohort members who were bringing up children on their own at 26 were mothers. The proportion of lone mothers (18 per cent of all women with children) was similar to the current national figures for all families with dependent children (Haskey, 1994). By comparison with partnered mothers, they tended to come from less advantaged home backgrounds themselves, and to have been less successful educationally - nearly one in five had left school with no qualifications.

From the information available, it was not possible to establish any direct link between these earlier characteristics and becoming a lone parent at age 26. What was clear, however, was the constraints they placed upon the young mothers' chances of achieving high level jobs and satisfactory living standards in 1990s Britain. Despite recent policy moves to remove lone mothers from dependence on state benefits, their level of participation in the labour market was far lower than that of their partnered peers, and just one in seven was in full-time work. Those that were in employment were more likely than partnered mothers to be in manual occupations. A further indicator of the relatively disadvantaged circumstances of the lone mothers was their concentration in social housing - two thirds were renting local authority or Housing Association accommodation, compared with less than a quarter of their married counterparts.

Thus, as other studies in this field have shown, women raising children on their own are among the most marginalised and vulnerable groups in our society, facing multiple obstacles to breaking out of a vicious circle of disadvantage (Burghes, 1993).

*Teenage parents*

All of the 1970 cohort members who had children by the age of 26 had become parents at a relatively young age by today's standards. However, one further group of particular interest were those who had had their first child while still in their teens. This is a life event associated with multiple disadvantage, including low socio-economic status and financial hardship in their families of origin, low educational attainment, and, as adults, poorer employment chances, higher likelihood of dependence on state benefits and lower levels of owner occupation (Kiernan, 1995; Burghes, 1995).

Teenage parents were identified by the age of the eldest biological child living in the cohort member's household at the time of the survey. This unavoidably missed out an unknown number of cohort members (especially young men) who had become parents as teenagers, but who were not living with their children at the time of the interview. From the information available it appeared that 17 per cent of the mothers and just eight per cent of the fathers had had their first child while in their teens.

There was little difference in the social class of origin of teenage parents and others, although, as already noted, *all* the cohort parents had had children at a relatively young age. There were variations, however, in educational attainment: more than three times as many teenage mothers had no qualifications, compared to those who had had their first child in their 20s.

Although we do not know at this stage what relationships the cohort members were in at the time of their child's conception and birth, the teenage mothers were far more likely than their older counterparts to be living as lone parents by the age of 26. One in four were alone with their child(ren), compared to about one in seven mothers who had their first child in their 20s, and a further small proportion (four per cent) were living, unpartnered, with their own parents. Most of the lone teenage mothers were single; just a small number had experienced separation or divorce. Although the majority of the partnered teenage mothers were married, they were also rather more likely than older mothers to be in a cohabiting relationship. Not surprisingly, almost all of the small group of men who reported having become fathers in their teens were living with a wife or partner.

Teenage mothers had similar levels of employment rates at 26 as those who had had their first child later, regardless of whether or not they were living with a partner at the time of the survey. However, early motherhood was associated with lower status occupations, with over half of the teenage mothers working in semi or unskilled manual occupations, compared to just over a quarter of the older mothers.

Teenage fathers, on the other hand, were particularly likely to be out of the labour market. Over a quarter were not in work (mostly unemployed) compared to less than one in ten of the older fathers. Of those in employment, very few (only four per cent) had professional or managerial jobs, compared with a quarter of those who had become fathers in their 20s.

As well as their disadvantaged labour market position, these young parents were also characterised by a less favourable position in the housing market. We have already seen that parents generally had lower rates of owner occupation than their childless counterparts; however, there were also differences linked to the age at which their first child had been born, with twice as many teenage parents living in social housing, and just half as many in owner occupation.

## The 'independent lifestyle'

The 26-year-olds who were living on their own at the time of the 1996 survey - especially the young women - were rather more likely than the cohort as a whole to have come from advantaged home backgrounds (Figure 4.3). They were also comparatively well-qualified: nearly a third of both men and women living alone had obtained a degree or equivalent, as against about one in five of the whole cohort (Figure 4.4). Their relatively high level of achievement was reflected in their occupational status: half had professional/managerial jobs compared with four out of ten in the cohort generally (Figure 4.5). A substantial minority of these independent 26-year-olds had already established themselves in the housing market - 40 per cent of the men and as many as 48 per cent of the women were owner occupiers at the time of the survey, similar to the figures for the cohort as a whole (Figure 4.6).

Yet there were also signs of less positive indicators among a minority in this group. The numbers reporting themselves as unemployed were relatively high - for women the highest of all groups, and for both sexes, those living alone contained the highest proportions recorded as long-term sick or disabled.

The other group living independently - those sharing accommodation with friends - were in certain respects even more favourably placed than those on their own. Among the men, twice as many as in any other group had fathers in professional/managerial occupations, and among the women the difference was even greater (Figure 4.3). This was also the group which had acquired the highest qualifications: more than half of the men and six out of ten women had obtained a degree or equivalent (Figure 4.4). The great majority of these cohort members were in full-time employment, and this group contained the highest proportion of all - two out of three - in professional or managerial positions (Figure 4.5). A considerable minority - more than in any other group - were still studying, with about one in 10 of both sexes reporting that they were still in full-time education.

Not surprisingly, relatively few of those living with friends had entered the housing market: two thirds of both men and women were living in privately rented accommodation - about four times as many as in the cohort as a whole.

These 'independent' groups were thus characterised by highly successful transitions to adulthood in terms of qualifications and career development. At the age of 26, they were still in the transitional phase of freedom and uncommitted relationships, and, perhaps as a direct result, appeared to have delayed moving on to cohabitation or marriage, and to the responsibilities of owner occupation.

*Living with parents*

In comparison with their counterparts who had remained single but were living 'independently', those cohort members who were living in their parental home had come from much less advantaged backgrounds in terms of their fathers' social class of occupation (Figure 4.3). They had also gained fewer qualifications than the other single cohort members. Just one in five of both men and women had a degree or equivalent, compared to more than half of those living with friends (Figure 4.4).

There was little indication that a disproportionate number of these cohort members had remained in their parents' home while they continued their education or training. Their labour market involvement, however, pointed to a relatively weak economic situation. As many as 10 per cent of the men living with their parents were unemployed at the time of the survey (Table 4.1). Those who were in work contained the highest proportion of any group who were in semi or unskilled jobs - nearly three times as many as those sharing accommodation with friends (Figure 4.5). Although the women living with their parents were no more likely than other groups to be out of the labour market, they, like their male counterparts, were less represented in high status occupations. Under a third were in professional/managerial posts, compared with half of the young women living alone and nearly two thirds of those sharing with friends. Clearly, such socio-economic indicators are likely to account only partially for the living arrangements of these 26-year-olds; social, emotional, and possibly health factors will also play a part. These findings do suggest, however, that for many of these young adults, lack of qualifications and consequent employment prospects had constrained their progress towards independent living.

## Conclusion

The 1996 survey has revealed great variations in the living arrangements and personal relationships of these 26-year-olds. We have identified a group of young men and women who are clearly 'getting on' in the 1990s sense of maximising their self-development. Prolonged education has equipped them with the qualifications needed to achieve high status occupations. This group have not yet, however, committed themselves in the field of personal relationships and family formation; they are more likely to be living independent lives in single person households or with friends.

Another major group consists of cohort members who have moved further on in the transition to adult life, having acquired a partner with whom they are living, either in cohabitation or marriage. Most are firmly established in the labour market, albeit in less elevated positions than their independent peers, and this is the group most likely to have got a foothold in owner occupation. However, for those who had also already become parents by age 26 - especially those in cohabiting unions - the picture was rather different. Both fathers and mothers had poorer qualifications, lower status jobs and were less likely to own their homes. Some analysts have suggested that early parenthood is an alternative source of adult identity among those whose lack of success in the education system makes high career aspirations unrealistic (Wilkinson, 1997). It is important to point out, however, that we do not know whether early parenthood was planned, or welcomed, and it would be wrong to make any value judgements about the 'success' or life satisfaction of this group on the basis of their relatively disadvantaged circumstances. What is also important is the social policy implications of these findings, in terms of the support needed for young families to enable them to provide an adequate material environment for their children.

Finally, we have identified several, relatively small, groups whose adult lives to date appear less promising. These include cohort members who had not yet made the transition to independent living, those who had already experienced the breakdown of a marriage, and those who had become parents at a very young age. Each of these groups was characterised by lack of educational qualifications, and a position in the labour market which was unlikely to guarantee self-sufficiency. As a consequence, they are particularly likely to be marginalised in a socio-economic context which denies access to independence and the mainstream culture for such groups, and fails to provide the support and alternative routes by which they could break out of their disadvantage.

# 5 Health and Health Behaviour

SCOTT M. MONTGOMERY and INGRID SCHOON

For a generation which has grown to adulthood during the 1980s and early 1990s, issues to do with health and health behaviour have been prominent for both positive and negative reasons. At one extreme, there has been unprecedented interest in promoting good health and a 'healthy lifestyle'; both in the public domain, with government reports such as 'The Health of the Nation' in 1992, and at the individual level with a widespread concern with personal fitness through, for example, exercise and healthy eating. At the other extreme, however, the last decade or so has had to confront the increasing risks to health posed by such threats as drugs, the HIV virus and numerous forms of environmental pollution. In addition, the most deprived locations and marginalised groups in Britain have experienced the re-emergence of conditions such as tuberculosis and rickets, which were, until recently, considered to be diseases consigned to history.

It has long been recognised that health varies according to social and economic circumstances. In general terms, greater material and psycho-social disadvantage is associated with greater risk of both mental and physical illness, although the mechanisms by which health is influenced are poorly understood. The majority of illnesses which vary as a function of socio-economic circumstances tend to have a long natural history and an ill-defined aetiology (Bartley et al., 1997). Some of this social patterning of health might be explained by a greater likelihood of environmental exposure to biological risk factors. However, while some environmental exposures may have an important role in determining the risk for some specific illnesses, socio-economic disadvantage is most likely to influence the course of many different diseases and health behaviour by damaging psychological well-being.

Socio-economic disadvantage may be defined in relative or absolute terms. Absolute disadvantage indicates an extreme state - for example, having so little money that it is impossible to buy sufficient food. Relative disadvantage, on the other hand, implies a contrast to other people in the same society; for instance, only having enough money to buy basic food, while the next door neighbour dines at the finest restaurants. Absolute disadvantage is associated with poverty.

A deterioration in both mental and physical health has been observed in people who have been forced to borrow money (White, 1991). Relative disadvantage may inflict damage through mechanisms such as increased social isolation and reduced frequency of leisure-time activities (Clarke, 1978). It has been suggested that the presence of a relatively disadvantaged group, or groups, within a population may reduce social cohesion, and this in turn may have negative consequences for the mental health of those in the disadvantaged groups (Wilkinson, 1996).

There is evidence to suggest that socio-economic disadvantage has a different impact, in terms of both mental and physical health, for men and women (Schoon and Montgomery, forthcoming). However, aspects of this difference may be distorted by the fact that men and women may be more or less susceptible to different diseases, or their risk of certain environmental exposures may differ. They may also have different symptoms, or report them differently. Despite the fact that, on average, women out-live men and have fewer accidents (at home, at work, on the road, at sport or elsewhere), many studies have found a tendency for women to report more illnesses and symptoms of disease than men of a similar age and background.

### Self-assessed general health status

**Table 5.1    General health by gender**

| Self-rated health | All | Men | Women |
|---|---|---|---|
| | % | % | % |
| Excellent | 35 | 38 | 33 |
| Good | 55 | 52 | 57 |
| Fair | 8 | 8 | 9 |
| Poor | 1 | 1 | 1 |
| n (100%) | (8957) | (4084) | (4873) |

As an indicator of their general health at age 26 years, the cohort members were asked to describe their overall health on a four point scale ranging from 'excellent' to 'poor'. The results of these self-ratings are presented in Table 5.1. The majority of the cohort members described their health as good or excellent. There were significant gender differences, insofar as more men reported that their health was excellent, while the same proportion of men and women (nine per cent in each case) claimed that it was just fair, or poor. When these figures were compared to those for 23-year-olds in the earlier 1958 cohort study, the health ratings of the 1970 cohort members were poorer for both men and women. However, the results for our 26-year-olds were similar to those found for the earlier cohort when they were aged 33.

**Mental health**

Mental health at age 26 years was investigated using the Malaise Inventory (Rutter et al., 1970; Grant et al., 1990), a 24 item checklist which measures emotional stress and associated somatic symptoms of depression. The Malaise Inventory score was divided into a 'normal' and a 'depressed' score, whereby a total of eight or more positive responses was used, as in previous studies (Richman, 1978; Rutter et al., 1970), to identify individuals at high risk of depression. While there was little difference in the proportions of men and women with fair or poor general health (both nine per cent), there was far more variation in relation to emotional state, with 18 per cent of women showing a tendency to depression, compared with just 12 per cent of men. We also found that the prevalence of depression had nearly doubled by comparison with the 1958 cohort when they were aged 23 (in 1981) and also when they were 33 (in 1991).

**Specific health problems**

The cohort members were also asked about 19 illnesses and symptoms that they may have had since they were 16 years of age. These ranged from potentially minor conditions, such as hay fever, to serious life threatening diseases like cancer (see Table 5.2).

Generally, we found a tendency for women to report more symptoms and illnesses than men. On average, women reported 2.57 symptoms and diseases, with only 14 per cent reporting none since they were 16 years old. In contrast, men reported an average of 1.78 symptoms, and 23 per cent said that they had never had any since the age of 16.

Three out of ten men and women reported suffering from hay fever, while about a fifth in each case had had wheezing or persistent joint or back pain. Nearly four out of ten women said that they suffered from migraine - twice as many as among the men. Women were also much more likely than men to have had eczema, and bladder or kidney problems. These gender differences highlight the importance of looking at risk factors and outcomes separately for men and women, a view which was reinforced when overall indicators of mental and physical health were considered.

**Table 5.2    Per cent with specific health problems since age 16 by gender**

| Health problem | All | | Male | | Female | |
|---|---|---|---|---|---|---|
| | *(n)* | *%* | *(n)* | *%* | *(n)* | *%* |
| Migraine | 2625 | 29 | 789 | 19 | 1836 | 37 |
| Hay fever | 2636 | 29 | 1190 | 29 | 1446 | 29 |
| Asthma | 1078 | 12 | 452 | 11 | 626 | 13 |
| Bronchitis | 538 | 6 | 195 | 5 | 343 | 7 |
| Wheezing | 1783 | 20 | 738 | 18 | 1045 | 21 |
| Skin problems: | | | | | | |
| eczema | 1404 | 16 | 452 | 11 | 952 | 19 |
| other | 1463 | 16 | 626 | 15 | 837 | 17 |
| Fits, epilepsy | 151 | 2 | 64 | 2 | 87 | 2 |
| Persistent joint or back pain | 1724 | 19 | 735 | 18 | 989 | 20 |
| Diabetes | 59 | 1 | 34 | 1 | 25 | <1 |
| Teeth, gums, mouth | 695 | 8 | 290 | 7 | 405 | 8 |
| Cancer | 36 | <1 | 15 | <1 | 21 | <1 |
| Stomach or digestive | 1010 | 11 | 425 | 10 | 585 | 12 |
| Bladder or kidney | 479 | 5 | 96 | 2 | 383 | 8 |
| Hearing difficulties | 280 | 3 | 143 | 3 | 137 | 3 |
| Other ear problems | 503 | 6 | 224 | 5 | 279 | 6 |
| Other health problems | 841 | 10 | 345 | 8 | 496 | 10 |

**Accumulation of risk**

A realistic description of the process by which socio-economic disadvantage results in excess mortality and morbidity is 'accumulation of risk'. As we have seen in previous chapters, those from a relatively disadvantaged family background were more likely to continue to experience socio-economic disadvantage as adults (Johnson and Reed, 1996). As disadvantage is associated with greater health risks, early disadvantage is likely to result in the accumulation of more health risks in both early and later life (Bartley et al., 1997). The factors indicating socio-economic circumstances in childhood and adult life that will be considered here are social class, based on father's occupation, and economic activity. Attained qualifications are also included in the analysis, as they mediate the effects of social circumstances in childhood and are also directly related to the risk of adult adversity.

Because many of the more serious physical illnesses have a long natural history, and tend to have their onset in middle or later life, our focus is primarily on the cohort members' psychological health, and self-reported health at 26, as these are more likely to show consistent socio-economic patterning at this relatively young age. Poor mental health or reduced psychological well-being are important outcomes in themselves. It is also likely that poor mental health, in terms of stress and depression, will be related to poor physical health in future years, as psychological stress has been shown to have negative consequences for physical wellbeing (Arnetz, et al., 1991; Kaplan, 1991). Stress can result in changes in the balance of the endocrine system (this controls the body, using chemical messengers in the blood stream), and these changes can increase the risk of developing certain diseases, including cardiovascular disease. The immune system, which is responsible for defending the body from infection, may be suppressed by stress and anxiety, thus increasing both an individual's risk of infection and the time it takes to clear.

### Social class at birth and health at age 26 years

The Registrar General's social class classification is widely used as an indicator of material and social circumstances, with a higher proportion of those in the lower categories experiencing some disadvantage. Here, two indicators of health at 26 - self-reported general health, and psychological health as measured by the Malaise Inventory - are examined in relation to father's social class when the cohort member was born.

**Figure 5.1    General health by social class in 1970**

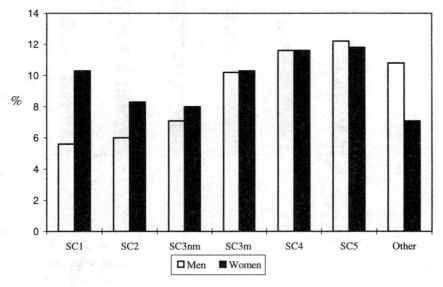

Figure 5.1 shows the relationship between social class at birth and self-reported general health some 26 years later. The answers to the general health question were dichotomised, so that those with either 'poor' or 'fair' health could be compared with the rest of the sample who described their health more positively. Overall, ten per cent of the cohort members reported fair or poor health. Among those in social class 1, the most privileged group, just eight per cent reported being in poor health, compared with 12 per cent in class 5. Interestingly, however, when the sexes were analysed separately, this relationship was statistically significant only for men. Only six per cent of men in class 1 reported poor health, compared with 11 per cent of those in class 5. Amongst women, however, the picture was less clear. Whilst the highest rates of poor health were found among those from manual backgrounds, that of women with fathers in the professions was also relatively high.

**Figure 5.2    Per cent depressed by social class: men and women**

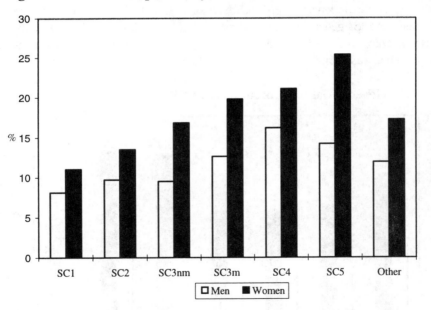

There was a marked relationship between social class at birth and depression at age 26, with 12 per cent men and 18 per cent women respectively falling into the depressed category (Figure 5.2). Among those with fathers in professional occupations, eight per cent of men and 11 per cent of women had a tendency to depression, compared with 15 per cent and 25 per cent respectively of those whose fathers had had unskilled jobs.

Clearly, class at birth is related to health many years later, but what sort of mechanisms can be used to explain this? Children who experience social and material disadvantage when they are young tend to carry the effects with them throughout their lives, with consequences in education, employment and family life (Pilling, 1990). This may operate through poorer educational attainment and, possibly, through other forms of reduced human capital (Bynner, forthcoming; Halsey et al., 1980). Poor social and material circumstances in childhood are associated with lower levels of subsequent educational attainment (Bynner and Parsons, this volume; Wadsworth, 1991). Those with poorer qualifications are at greater risk of subsequent labour market disadvantage, including an increased risk of experiencing unemployment (Glyn, 1995; Joshi and Paci, this volume; Payne et al., 1994).

*Qualifications and health at age 26*

If the relationship between social and material disadvantage in childhood and adult ill-health is mediated, in part, by poor educational attainment, we would expect to see a relationship between educational attainment and the health outcome variables at age 26 years. Here, qualifications have been grouped into the five levels used previously.

**Figure 5.3    General health by highest qualification: men and women**

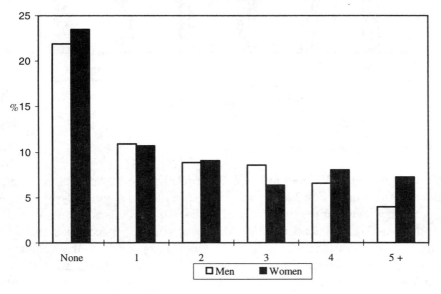

Figure 5.3 illustrates the strong relationship between qualifications attained and subsequent self-reported general health. Overall, those who had no qualifications were four times more likely to report poor general health (23 per cent) than those with the highest level qualifications (six per cent). The pattern was the same for men and women. A similarly strong relationship between qualifications and depression at age 26 years is demonstrated by figure 5.4. The tendency reported earlier for more women than men to experience depression was evident at each level of qualifications. What was particularly striking was the very high proportion of women with no qualifications who indicated that they were depressed (37 per cent).

**Figure 5.4    Per cent depressed by highest qualification: men and women**

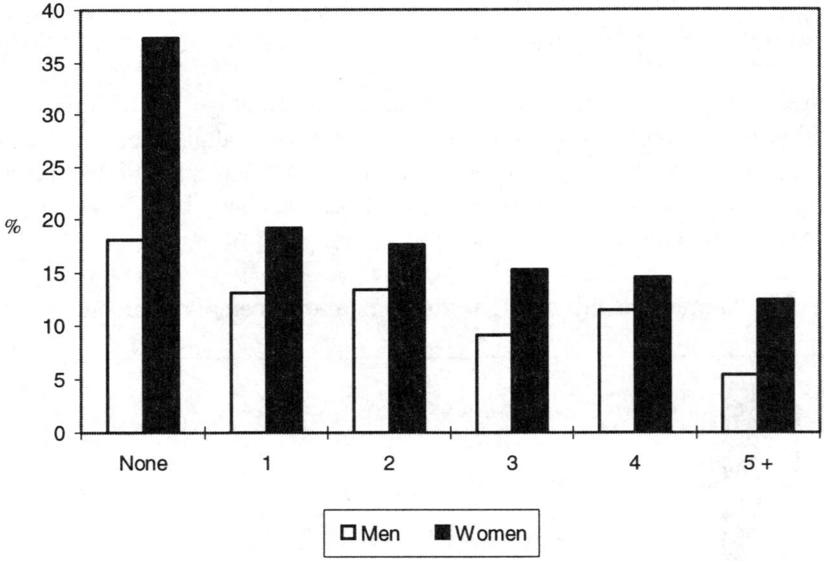

*Economic activity and health at age 26*

Educational failure alone does not explain the relationship between adversity in childhood and worse adult health, but poorer qualifications are likely to be an important link between the two. Lack of, or low, qualifications are associated with a greater risk of labour market disadvantage and an increased risk of unemployment, particularly for men (Glyn, 1995; Joshi and Paci, this volume). This is partly because men with lower levels of educational attainment tend also to be less skilled workers (Nickell and Bell, 1995). Men with lower levels of qualifications are far less likely to augment their skills through training than more qualified men (Bynner and Parsons, this volume; Green, 1994), and employers tend to be less likely to invest in training those without qualifications. Men with lower levels of skill found themselves at an increasing disadvantage in the labour market in the 1980s, due to both economic and industrial change. The proliferation of new technology  resulted in a reduction in skill content of lower skill jobs and, more significantly, a reduction in the share of such jobs in the labour market. At the same time, the skill content and labour market share of high skill jobs increased (Glyn,1995). This was reflected in an expansion of job opportunities requiring higher levels of qualifications and, in real terms, a contraction of the number of jobs requiring fewer qualifications (Gittleman, 1994). In times of recession, employers are more likely to continue to employ the highly skilled employees (who can also undertake less skilled jobs). Those men with lower skill levels tend to have a 'weaker attachment to firms'(Nickell and Bell, 1995), and for this reason have a far higher turnover rate. As a consequence of this, far more of them experience unemployment. Once unemployed, the men with lowest skill levels may have less incentive to return to work due to low wage levels: Nickell and Bell (1995) observed that in countries without unemployment benefit systems, the uneducated are less able to cope with unemployment and are forced into jobs with low pay.

Qualifications are thus likely to influence health through an individual's relative success or failure in the labour market. We examined the relationship between economic activity  and health outcomes at age 26, with the cohort members' main economic activity categorised as: working full-time; working part-time; not working; and staying at home (Figure 5.5).

**Figure 5.5    General health by main economic activity: men and women**

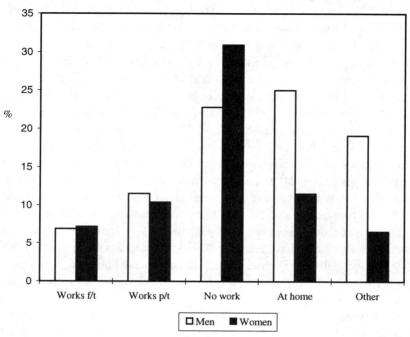

For both men and women, the economic activity associated with the lowest risk of poor general health was working full-time. Only seven per cent of both men and women in this category reported poor health (Figure 5.5). Only a very small number of men (12) said that they were out of the labour market 'at home', and so it is not possible to draw conclusions about the findings relating to this group. By contrast, the worst general health was associated with unemployment, and in this group, 31 per cent of women and 23 per cent of men reported poor health. For women, while staying at home was somewhat better than unemployment, it was still significantly associated with poor general health.

**Figure 5.6    Per cent depressed by main economic activity: men and women**

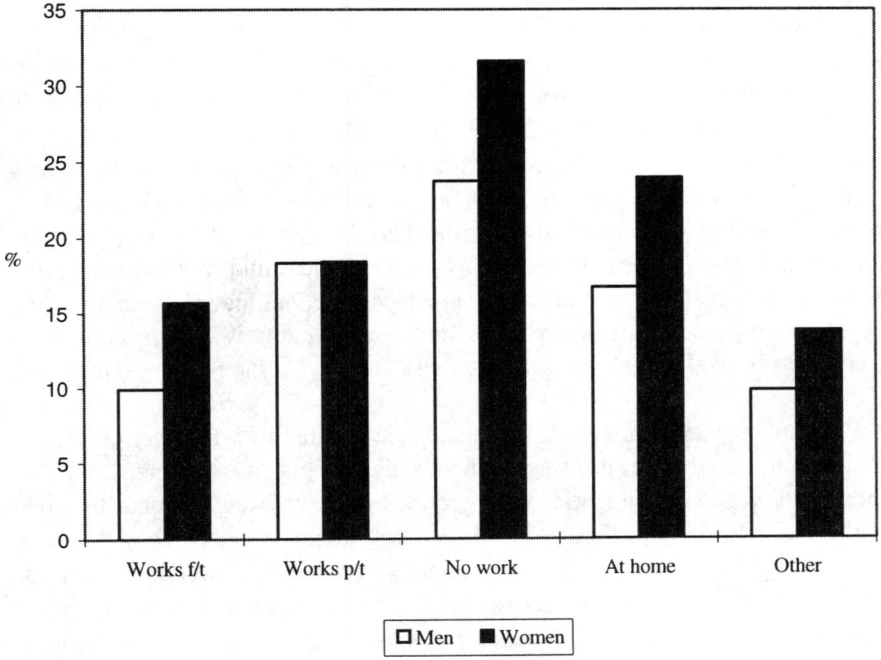

Similar results were found for the relationship between economic activity and depression at age 26 years (Figure 5.6). Unemployment was also associated with the greatest risk of depression: within this group, 32 per cent of women and 24 per cent of men were depressed. Again, for women, being a home-maker was significantly associated with a tendency to depression.

**Health-related behaviour**

In recent years there have been several attempts, through government campaigns, to increase awareness of 'healthy lifestyles'. These campaigns have suggested behavioural changes, including dietary changes, less smoking and moderate drinking. Many positive health behaviours, however, are more apparent in the more advantaged groups. Cigarette smoking, for example, is classbound, with those from manual social class backgrounds more likely to become smokers and less likely to give it up (Montgomery et al., forthcoming). In the present survey of the 1970 cohort, health behaviour was assessed by the respondents' self-reported view of their body weight, and their drinking and smoking behaviour.

*Obesity*

The growing prevalence of obesity and excess weight in all age groups in our society is a trend which is arousing increasing attention and concern. Studies have shown that obesity is linked with a higher risk of heart disease, and also to social class background. However, the obesity-class gradient does not develop until middle-age, so our cohort members were too young, at 26, to clearly observe the relationship between obesity and disadvantage. Independently of age, though, some people, particularly women, may be depressed because they are overweight. Stress has been linked both with weight loss and weight gain: severe depression may result in weight change in either direction. Indeed, weight cycling (an alternating pattern of weight loss and weight gain) is associated with a number of physical symptoms which are risk factors for later illness (Bosello et al., 1993).

Cohort members were asked to indicate whether they felt very or slightly underweight, about the right weight, slightly overweight or overweight. For our analysis, the response categories were grouped into: overweight, about the right weight and underweight. Figure 5.7 shows that women were twice as likely to feel overweight (16 per cent) as underweight (eight per cent) while for men, the reverse was the case (seven per cent as against 15 per cent). There was a marked relationship between depression and a perception that weight was not optimal: some 23 per cent of depressed women and 11 per cent of depressed men describe themselves as overweight, while 12 per cent of depressed women and 21 per cent of depressed men said that they were underweight. This confirms the widespread assumption that consciousness of a less than ideal body image is associated with depression, especially among women.

**Figure 5.7    Self-perceived weight by employment status: men and women**
**a) Overweight**

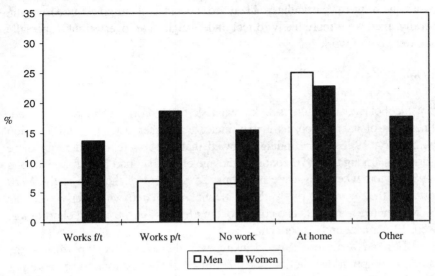

**b) Underweight**

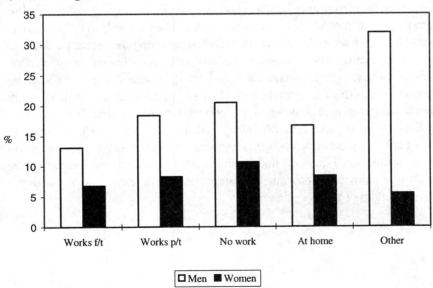

There was also a connection between perception of own weight and economic activity: those activities described above as linked with a higher risk of depression were also associated with a higher risk of self-reported obesity in women and lower body mass in men (Figure 5.7). Women at home were more likely to feel overweight than women in or out of work, though it was women out of work who were particularly likely to consider themselves underweight. Generally, men were more likely to feel underweight than overweight, especially if they were out of work.

*Drinking*

Heavy alcohol consumption is a known risk factor for several diseases, but abstinence is of interest too, as it may indicate a higher risk of social isolation (Montgomery, 1996). Our findings showed that there were considerably more non-drinkers among the 1970 cohort at the age of 26 than had been found among the 1958 cohort when they were 33. Some 25 per cent of the men in the 1970 cohort said they never or rarely drank alcohol, compared with nearly twice as many women (45 per cent). The corresponding figures for the 1958 cohort at age 33 were 14 per cent and 29 per cent.

For our analyses, heavy drinking was defined as the top fifth of the alcohol consumption distribution (24 units of alcohol consumption or more per week). Heavy drinking at this level was reported by 29 per cent of men, but only four per cent of women in the 1970 cohort. Depression seemed to accentuate this pattern to some extent: depressed men were more likely to be heavy drinkers (35 per cent) or non-drinkers (21 per cent). Depression among men is thus associated with both a greater risk of heavier drinking and of abstention from alcohol. Depressed women were also more likely to be non-drinkers (32 per cent), but no more likely than others to drink heavily (four per cent) (Figure 5.8). Looking at the relationship between drinking and economic activity we find that men were most likely to be non-drinkers when they had no work, and women when they were at home, or working part-time. The group of men 'at home' was too small to draw conclusions. Heavier drinking, on the other hand, was most likely among the men in employment, possibly indicating the role of income in sustaining a persistent pattern of heavier drinking.

**Figure 5.8   Drinking by employment status: men and women**
a) Non drinking

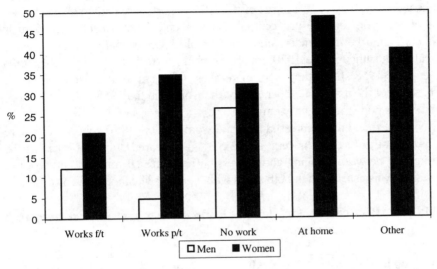

b) Heavy drinking

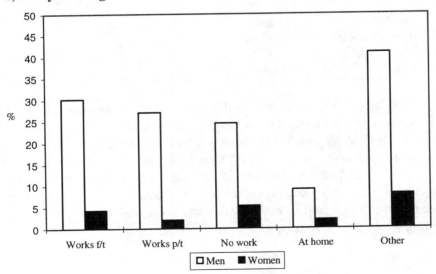

*Smoking*

At the age of 26, nearly two thirds of the 1970 cohort were non-smokers (61 per cent of the men and 65 per cent of the women), 27 per cent were regular smokers, and the remainder said they smoked occasionally. These figures indicate that although the 1970 cohort members were less likely to drink than those in the 1958 study, they were more likely to be smokers. At the age of 33, 68 per cent of the men and 69 per cent of the women in the 1958 cohort had been identified as non-smokers or ex-smokers.

We found that depressed men and women in the 1970 cohort were more likely than others to be smokers (Table 5.3). It appeared, too, that whereas the relationship between drinking and depression had differed for men and women, depression was associated in both sexes with a greater likelihood of smoking.

**Table 5.3    Per cent smoking levels: depressed men and women compared with total sample**

| Smoking level | All | Depressed Men | Depressed Women |
|---|---|---|---|
| | % | % | % |
| Non-smoker | 61 | 42 | 50 |
| Occasional smoker | 10 | 12 | 10 |
| Regular smoker | 29 | 46 | 40 |
| *n (100%)* | *(6940)* | *(351)* | *(730)* |

Figure 5.9 shows that most of the regular smokers were unemployed or at home. This was not surprising, as smoking has been identified as a relief, or coping mechanism for people who have unsatisfactory circumstances, such as those associated with unemployment (Montgomery et al., forthcoming). For women, being at home at the age of 26 was closely linked with young motherhood and having young dependent children (Ferri and Smith, this volume). In many cases, this would be likely to represent a stressful situation, for which smoking would provide some relief.

**Figure 5.9   Smoking by main economic activity: men and women**
**a) Regular smoking**

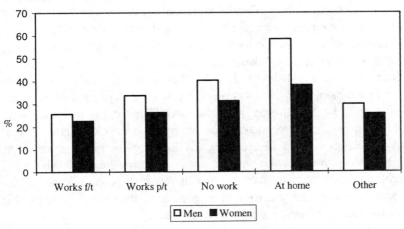

**b) Non smoking**

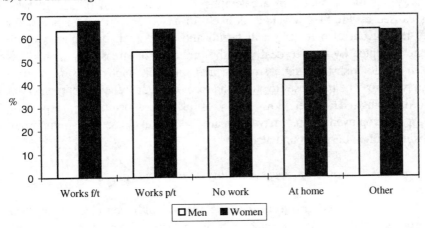

## Summary and conclusion

The results of this analysis of the health and health behaviour of the 1970 cohort have revealed a clear link between social disadvantage, past and present, and physical and emotional well-being. There were also differences between men and women, particularly in respect of depression and health behaviour.

In comparison to the more privileged social groups, we found that more of the 26-year-olds from a lower social class background - especially men - described their general health as poor. While men in general were less likely than women to suffer from depression, both men and women from the manual social classes were more likely to be depressed than their peers from more advantaged homes. Likewise, more men and women with no qualifications described their general health as poor, and more showed symptoms of depression, than was the case among cohort members who had obtained qualifications. In terms of their current economic activity, we also found that unemployed cohort members were less healthy, and more depressed, than cohort members in full-time employment.

Men were more likely to describe themselves as underweight than women, who were more likely to report being overweight. Depressed women, and those who were at home full-time, were the most likely to say that they were overweight. Men were also more likely than women to be smokers, and to drink more heavily. Depressed men were particularly likely to describe themselves as underweight, and to drink heavily; while unemployed men were also likely to feel underweight, and to be regular smokers. A relatively high proportion of heavier drinkers was found among the men in employment, indicating, perhaps, the importance of an earned income to fund heavier drinking.

The stress associated with disadvantage in childhood and adult life may be a very significant factor in accelerating the accumulation of health risks. Stress caused by life-time adversity is likely to have consequences not just for mental health, but also for physical health and other adult outcomes. Coping strategies adopted by men to deal with the problems of stress may themselves represent health risks: cigarette smoking and relatively high levels of alcohol consumption may be responses to stress that provide acute relief (Montgomery et al., forthcoming). However, low levels of alcohol consumption, especially amongst unemployed men, may indicate social exclusion, as important socialising is often based around alcohol.

*Disadvantage as a cause of excess mortality and morbidity*

The 1970 cohort members seemed to be more health conscious than their counterparts in the 1958 cohort, since a higher proportion stated that they were non-drinkers and non-smokers. This might suggest that the considerable amount of campaigning against alcohol and nicotine directed at young people in recent years has paid some dividends. However, the 1970 cohort members appeared to be more depressed and in poorer general health than those in the 1958 cohort. This may indicate an alarming trend in which the mental health of British young people is worsening over successive generations. It is unlikely that 1970 cohort members are simply more innately prone to illness than a cohort born 12 years earlier; what is more likely is that changing environmental and societal factors have resulted in a higher proportion of the 1970 cohort having poorer health by the age of 26. As social and economic factors are clearly important in determining health risk, could the changes which have set the scene for the survey reported in this book be responsible for the apparently growing number of young people whose long-term health is at risk? It does indeed seem likely that widening social inequality will result in a parallel widening of health inequality. Significant social variation in health among these young people will be revealed in due course by differentials in illness and early death. Unnecessary illness and suffering linked to social inequality may be exacerbated for those who entered young adulthood at a time when the labour market was uncertain, and competition for good jobs was fierce. At the same time, the real value of state benefits had been eroded, so that many would experience relative, and perhaps absolute, poverty. The best medicine for many of the illnesses with a psychosocial origin would be the introduction of measures to reduce socio-economic disadvantages.

To establish patterns of causality to explain why disadvantaged groups tend to have worse health, it will be necessary to study the life-long accumulation of health risks, and their interactions with each other, as well as with other personal and environmental characteristics. An examination of the life-long continuity of disadvantage that many people experience is likely to provide the most complete explanation of the link between disadvantage and ill-health. It can be misleading only to consider adult (or current) circumstances, without considering childhood or previous disadvantage. The association of adverse socio-economic circumstances with the accumulation of biological risk factors can start in early life, and continue throughout adulthood (Bartley et al., 1997). Children from relatively disadvantaged backgrounds are more likely to be in poorer health as adults. Their childhood circumstances may have made them more vulnerable to future illness (Montgomery et al., 1996, 1995) and this childhood vulnerability has been shown to be associated with socio-economic disadvantage that continues into early adulthood. Poorer educational performance is also more likely to result in continuing disadvantage, such as unemployment (Montgomery et al., 1996). It might be argued that pre-existing chronic illness might have resulted in the relationships between poorer qualifications and economic inactivity with worse health at age 26 years. However, this is not the case. Exclusion of all cohort members with a limiting chronic illness or disability did not significantly change these relationships.

The variability of the processes by which risks to health are accumulated throughout life indicates that there will be considerable variation in the timing of the onset and nature of any morbidity. Mental health may deteriorate rapidly during a spell of very high stress, but physical health may be slowly eroded over many years. Deterioration in mental health, due to factors such as unemployment, tends not to continue indefinitely: usually, mental health begins to improve again due to habituation to the state of being unemployed, although it may not recover completely (Banks and Ullah, 1988). Re-employment to a 'good' job is also likely to increase psychological well-being after a spell of unemployment. Disadvantage and stress do not necessarily result in depression, disease and an early death, as there are many factors that protect against these outcomes. Social support from families and friends may be particularly effective in preventing adverse physical and mental consequences due to disadvantage and stress. Our only hope of fully understanding the processes that lead to social patterning of health and illness is through detailed examination of longitudinal data, such as that offered by the 1970 British Cohort Study.

# 6   Views, Voting and Values

RICHARD D. WIGGINS, JOHN BYNNER and SAMANTHA PARSONS

## Introduction

In Chapter 1, the possible emergence of a new politics was signalled, in which the 1970 cohort was thought to be the vanguard. At the time the cohort was leaving education in the mid to late 1980s, political apathy was widespread, and cynicism about politics and the motives of politicians the norm. However, there were signs that the feelings were directed largely towards the main political parties. Surveys of young people at the time showed that issues concerning race, gender relations and the environment aroused the strongest feelings among young people, party politics the weakest feelings of all. Where there were party political affiliations, these tended to be largely a reflection of parents' views (Banks et al., 1992). Although the Green Party picked up large numbers of votes from young people in the 1988 elections for the European Parliament, this success for 'alternative politics' was not sustained. In so far as young people participated in politics at all, it was in terms of the traditional party divide - encouraged to take part by some of the events at the time which affected young people most directly. The Conservative government's promotion in the 1980s of such measures as YTS, and the 'poll tax', both of which impacted on young people, consistently pushed them in an anti-government direction. But the general lack of attention to young people's concerns by the opposition parties meant that little political capital was gained from their disaffection. This was the generation that grew up with Thatcherism, and from the age of nine never experienced anything else.

But this takes us to some of the many paradoxes that emerge in the study of politics (Heath and Topf, 1987). Despite the general lack of interest in politics among young people, as they get older more of them express an intention to vote. Moreover, although in the 1980s this intention was marginally more common among the most educated, young people in all groups subscribed to it. This was a lot less true of political interest, which remained much more the territory of those engaged in further and higher education. Thus, exposure to the world of youth training, employment and unemployment, and a rapidly disappearing youth labour market, far from heightening political interest seemed, if anything, to dampen it. This is in line with what has been described as the 'resource model' of politics, whereby those who, through education, think they can influence events, express the most interest in doing so, while those on the 'coal face', confronting political issues on a daily basis, remain largely unmoved by them (Marsh, 1990; Bynner and Ashford, 1994).

Perhaps the more encouraging side of the picture was the failure of alternative politics of a more menacing kind to take off. Although, in the early 1980s, there had been some signs of increased support among young people for the National Front (Cochrane and Billig, 1982), this failed to materialise any further into an endorsement of fascism. Only a tiny proportion of the young people in the four areas of Britain studied in the ESRC 16-19 Initiative, reported affiliation to the parties of the far right (Bynner and Ashford, 1994).

In this chapter, we move on in the cohort members' lives to an examination of their views and actions at the age of 26. To what extent were their views much the same as those of the earlier generation and how were they differentiated by the major structural factors of class, education and gender? Was there mass abstention from politics among 26-year-olds and, if there was, who was doing it? Who was interested in politics? Which party was attracting most political support?

## Views and values

The questionnaire contained 17 statements of everyday opinions, to each of which the respondent was asked to indicate their agreement or disagreement. These ranged from concerns about law and order - such as 'people who break the law should be given stiffer sentences' - to responsibility for household management, for example: 'when both partners work full-time, the man should take an equal share of the domestic chores'. All of the statements were accompanied by five response categories: 'strongly agree', 'agree', 'uncertain', 'disagree' or 'strongly disagree' - scored 1, 2, 3, 4, 5 respectively. All of these statements had been used previously, in the 1991 survey of the 1958 cohort at the age of 33 (Wiggins and Bynner, 1993).

In addition to the opinion statements, respondents were also asked a number of questions inviting them to say how they felt about their lives and themselves. For example, they were asked to make assessments of their standard of living compared with that of others, and to indicate the extent to which they felt a sense of control over what happened in life (self-efficacy), by endorsing one of two statements as true for them: 'I usually have a free choice and control over my life' versus 'Whatever I do has no real effect on what happens to me'. Their satisfaction with life was assessed from the question, 'How satisfied or dissatisfied are you about the way your life has turned out so far?'. Respondents had to place a mark along a visual scale of satisfaction ranging from 'completely dissatisfied' (score 0) to 'completely satisfied' (score 9). Finally, to complete the picture, their identification with a religion, and their political preferences and views about voting were sought. Interest in politics was assessed on a four point scale: 'very interested', 'fairly interested', 'not very interested', 'not at all interested'. Voting intention was elicited by asking respondents to indicate which political party they would vote for if there was a general election tomorrow.

*The climate of opinion*

The opinion statements help us to gain an overall picture of the climate of opinion among the cohort members, and some insights into changes since the 1991 survey of 33-year-olds. To simplify the picture, the statistical technique of factor analysis was used to help identify groups of opinions which shared something in common, i.e. agreement with one statement in the group was likely to be accompanied by agreement with other statements (Kline, 1994). For example, people who agreed strongly 'that couples who have children should not separate' were also likely to agree strongly that 'marriage is for life'. Such groupings of opinions can be identified with broader dispositions - attitude factors or dimensions - each of which can be labelled to summarise the content of the constituent opinion statements. These labels serve to flag up underlying sets of values - left/right, for example. Again, to simplify the presentation of findings, for much of the analysis the individual items are replaced by summary variables, the scores for which were obtained by averaging the scores on the individual items. We will refer to these new (more reliable) variables as *attitude scales* (McKennell, 1977). After carrying out an exploratory factor analysis, *five* separate attitude scales were constructed (see Appendix 2). They encompassed all of the original 17 statements and were labelled:

- *political cynicism*
- *support for sex equality*
- *support for law and order*
- *support for traditional marital values*
- *support for work ethic*

Table 6.1 lists all the opinion statements, grouped in terms of the five attitude scales, together with the percentages agreeing and disagreeing with each statement. The column on the right-hand side gives the percentages who *strongly agreed* or *strongly disagreed*; i.e. they felt most strongly about the issue.

## Table 6.1    Views of the whole sample

|  | Agree | Uncertain | Disagree | Strongly agree/ disagree |
|---|---|---|---|---|
|  | % | % | % | % |
| **Political cynicism** |  |  |  |  |
| None of the political parties would do anything to benefit me | 21 | 39 | 40 | 8 |
| Politicians are mainly in politics for their own benefit and not for the benefit of the community | 44 | 33 | 23 | 11 |
| It does not really make a difference which political party is in power in Britain | 26 | 27 | 47 | 17 |
| **Support for sex equality** |  |  |  |  |
| There should be more women bosses in important jobs in business and industry | 68 | 22 | 10 | 20 |
| Men and women should all have the chance to do the same kind of work | 90 | 5 | 5 | 40 |
| When both partners work full-time, the man should take an equal share of domestic chores | 96 | 2 | 2 | 53 |
| If a child is ill and both partners are working it should usually be the mother who takes time off work to look after the child | 21 | 18 | 61 | 16 |
| **Support for law and order** |  |  |  |  |
| People who break the law should be given stiffer sentences | 72 | 21 | 7 | 31 |
| For some crimes the death penalty is the most appropriate sentence | 69 | 12 | 19 | 48 |
| Censorship of films and magazines is necessary to uphold moral standards | 63 | 14 | 23 | 18 |
| The law should be obeyed even if a particular law is wrong | 57 | 23 | 20 | 11 |
| **Support for traditional marital values** |  |  |  |  |
| Couples who have children should not separate | 16 | 27 | 58 | 12 |
| Marriage is for life | 73 | 15 | 13 | 35 |
| Divorce is too easy to get these days | 51 | 29 | 20 | 15 |
| **Support for the work ethic** |  |  |  |  |
| If I didn't like a job I'd pack it in, even if there was no other job to go to | 13 | 16 | 71 | 24 |
| Having almost any job is better than being unemployed | 66 | 12 | 22 | 26 |
| Government should redistribute income from the better off to those who are less well off | 41 | 24 | 35 | 20 |

*n (100%) = 9003*

*Political cynicism*  Of the three statements under this heading, the belief that politicians are mainly in politics for their own benefit was endorsed by over two fifths of the respondents. There was more ambivalence about whether there were any personal benefits to be gained from any political party, and whether it mattered much which party was in power - one fifth and one quarter respectively took the cynical view, with large proportions saying they were uncertain. These figures correspond quite closely to those for the same statement when put to 33-year-olds in the 1958 cohort study survey, except that five per cent more of our younger cohort agreed that politicians were in politics mainly for their own benefit. It seems that although there was distrust of politicians personally this did not extend to same extent to the political process, which was still seen by a sizeable proportion as capable of delivering benefits.

*Support for sex equality* The figures suggest overwhelming support for equality between the sexes. Hardly anybody disagreed that men and women should be able to do the same kind of work or that men and women should take an equal share of domestic work. There was some dissent about the statement that there should be more women bosses in the top jobs in business and industry; however, over 68 per cent agreed. And opinions differed about whether, when a child was sick and both parents were working, the *mother* should take time off to look after the child; nonetheless, 61 per cent *disagreed*. Notably, for every one of these statements, more 1970 cohort members than their counterparts in the 1958 cohort endorsed the pro-sex equality position. This points to a small but consistent shift in the younger cohort towards support for more equality between the sexes.

*Support for law and order* There was majority support for a tougher approach to law and order issues. Seven out of ten respondents thought that sentencing should be 'stiffer', and a similar proportion supported the death penalty for some crimes. More surprisingly, perhaps, censorship of films and magazines received majority endorsement, just under two thirds agreeing that this was needed to uphold moral standards. Just over half went so far as to agree that the law should be obeyed even if it was wrong. Again for every one of these statements, endorsement was greater by a few per cent than in the 1958 cohort. Thus, despite the more liberal views that were evident in relation to sex equality, there appeared to be a hardening of views about crime and punishment, with a generally more punitive stance being the norm.

*Support for traditional marital values* These statements elicited what appeared to be contradictory opinions. Thus, although nearly three quarters agreed that marriage was for life, and half agreed that divorce was too easy to get these days, less than one in five followed these opinions up by agreeing that people should not separate if they have children. It seems that belief in marriage as an institution was countered by the even stronger belief that in certain circumstances it may be in the children's and the parents' interest for the parents to split up. Thus, support for the traditional conception of the permanence of marriage was tempered by the modern conception of individual interests and rights. The first of these statements produced the biggest shift of all between the two surveys. Only *three fifths* of the 1958 cohort agreed that marriage is for life compared with nearly *three quarters* of the 1970 cohort - a move towards marriage. For the statements about separation and divorce, however, much the same proportions shared the same position in the two surveys.

*Support for the work ethic* These statements reflect on current debates about the extent to which new generations are rejecting the work ethic in favour of self-actualisation through other means - consumption in place of production? There were few signs of a general rejection of work as an ideal, though a degree of ambivalence about it was also apparent. Hence, two thirds agreed that having any job was better than being unemployed, and only 13 per cent said they would pack a job in if they did not like it, even if there was no other job to go to. Rising consciousness of the declining job market perhaps lay behind the even greater commitment to employment among the 1970 cohort than among their counterparts in the 1958 cohort, of whom only one half agreed that having any job was better than being unemployed; two thirds of the 1970 cohort took this view. And more of the 1970 cohort said they *would not* pack a job in if they did not like it: 71 per cent compared with 64 per cent. This suggests that, if anything, the 1970 cohort was *more* committed to work than the older 1958 cohort. Notably too, on another issue, which was linked only loosely to the others in this group, fewer of the 1970 cohort, 41 per cent, thought the government should re-distribute money from the wealthy to the most needy, whereas 50 per cent of the 1958 cohort took this view.

## Most important issues?

A final feature of the climate of opinion is the importance cohort members attached to particular issues. We get an indication of this from the percentages who gave the *extreme* responses to each statement, i.e. the percentages who *strongly agreed* or *strongly disagreed*. The last column in table 6.1 gives these percentages. We use them to rank the relative importance of the statements to the cohort members.

The statements that came top of the ranking were two of those to do with, on the one hand, liberal views about sex equality, and on the other, traditional views about law and order. First was the issue of men taking an equal share with women of household chores; it was followed closely by the appropriateness of the death penalty for some crimes. These were followed by the statement about men and women's right to do the same kind of work, and then the question of the need for stiffer sentences for people who break the law. Whether marriage was for life came next, then the three statements about the work ethic and whether there should be more women bosses. The statements arousing least passion were about politicians and the political parties, and whether the law should always be obeyed.

## Who holds the different social attitudes?

To investigate the extent to which attitudes differed, or were the same, across different sections of the cohort, we compared the mean attitude scores for different groups, defined by such characteristics as gender, educational level, employment situation, partnership status and parental status.

### Gender

Figure 6.1 shows that, compared with men, women respondents tended to be slightly less cynical about politics, to be stronger supporters of sex equality, and law and order and to support the work ethic more. On the other hand, they were no more committed than their male counterparts to support for marriage. This reveals a shift across the generations, since larger numbers of women than men in the 1958 cohort study supported marriage.

**Figure 6.1  Mean scores on attitude scales: comparisons between men and women**

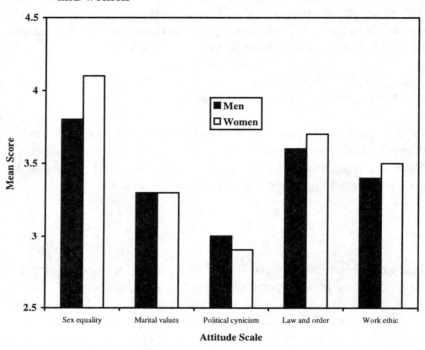

*Highest educational qualification*

Educational background showed stronger relationships with the attitude scales (Figures 6.2). With respect to support for sex equality, the mean scores *increased* steadily as the level of educational qualification rose. Conversely, the degree of expressed political cynicism *decreased* as the level of educational qualification improved. The most politically cynical were those with no educational qualifications at all. While the existence of such linear trends is not so noticeable among the other scales, those with the highest qualifications stood out as those who were *least* likely to give unquestioning support for law and order or to support traditional marital values; those who had CSE level or equivalent qualifications were the most in favour of law and order.

**Figure 6.2  Mean scores on attitude scales: comparisons by highest academic qualification at 26**

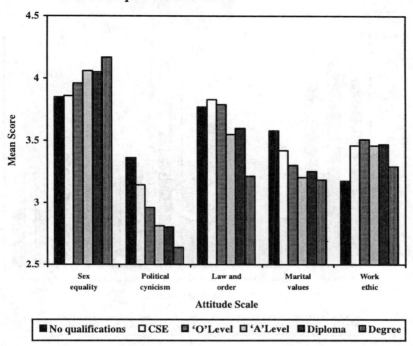

*Employment status*

Those respondents still in full-time education at age 26 were almost all in higher education. Therefore their employment status was largely a reflection of the high qualifications they held. It is not surprising therefore that they tended to be the *least* politically cynical and the *most* likely to support sex equality (Figure 6.3). Those in full-time employment or describing themselves as being 'at home' scored highest on support for the work ethic, and law and order. The unemployed were the least supportive of the work ethic. There were barely any differences in support for traditional marital values.

**Figure 6.3   Mean scores on attitude scales: comparisons by employment status at 26**

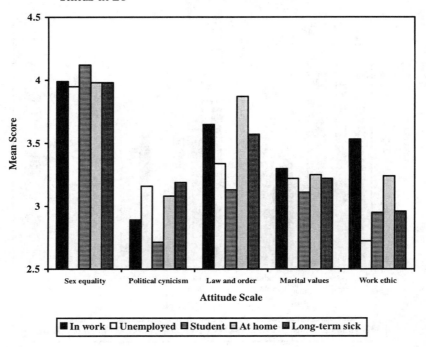

*Partnership status*

Cohort members' partnership status related to some attitudes but not others. Figure 6.4 shows that support for sex equality and political cynicism were largely unconnected with living arrangements. The strongest relationship was for law and order, where the married and divorced groups took the toughest line. The other attitude which divided the groups, but less strongly, was the 'work ethic', which this time attracted the most support from the married group. Finally, as we might expect, attitudes to marriage divided the groups in terms of whether they were in partnerships or married. The currently married group was the most committed to the traditional view of marriage, whereas the divorced group was the least supportive of it. Those who were single and those who were cohabiting fell in between.

**Figure 6.4   Mean scores on attitude scales: comparisons by partnership status**

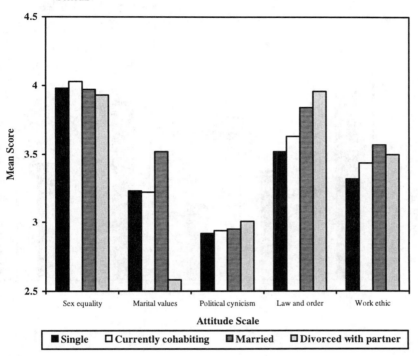

*Parental status*

By the age of 26, one in five of the men and one in three of the women in the 1970 cohort had become parents. The relationships between the attitudes and parental status were less clear cut. As Figure 6.5 shows, the only scale which strongly differentiated the groups was support for law and order, with the cohort members who were parents endorsing this position more than those who were childless. The other differences were barely significant. Marginally more people with children endorsed traditional marital values and were politically cynical, and slightly fewer supported sex equality.

**Figure 6.5    Mean scores on attitude scales: comparisons for those with or without children**

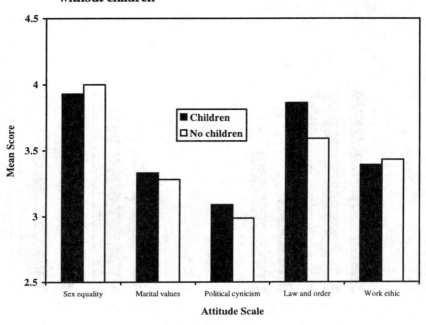

## Personal identity

The social attitudes we have considered so far may be seen as a reflection of the social part of the cohort members' identities, i.e. how they represent themselves to other people. The other major facet of identity is what people think about themselves. In particular the cohort members were asked to make assessments of their standard of living, the extent to which they felt a sense of control over what happened in life and their satisfaction with the way their lives had turned out so far. Finally, another facet of personal identity is whether people identify with a religion. We also asked cohort members if they belonged to any religion: 39 per cent said they did.

*Self attitudes*

**Table 6.2**    **Self attitudes and religious affiliation by sex, highest qualification, employment status, partnership and parent status**

| Characteristic | Standard of living better | Feels in control of life | Satisfied with life | Belongs to a religion | n (100%) |
|---|---|---|---|---|---|
| | % | % | % | % | |
| **Sex** | | | | | |
| Male | 54 | 93 | 43 | 32 | *(4102)* |
| Female | 50 | 94 | 48 | 44 | *(4901)* |
| **Highest qualification** | | | | | |
| None | 39 | 82 | 31 | 27 | *(487)* |
| CSE | 44 | 91 | 39 | 33 | *(1462)* |
| 'O'Level | 51 | 94 | 46 | 38 | *(3446)* |
| 'A'Level | 56 | 96 | 49 | 46 | *(894)* |
| Diploma | 56 | 97 | 45 | 46 | *(374)* |
| Degree | 65 | 97 | 53 | 46 | *(1736)* |
| **Employment status** | | | | | |
| In work | 56 | 95 | 48 | 39 | *(7266)* |
| Unemployed | 28 | 83 | 21 | 30 | *(384)* |
| Student | 39 | 96 | 48 | 48 | *(240)* |
| At home | 36 | 88 | 40 | 35 | *(690)* |
| Long-term sick | 33 | 70 | 29 | 46 | *(137)* |
| **Partnership status** | | | | | |
| Single | 47 | 95 | 35 | 40 | *(3704)* |
| Currently cohabiting | 56 | 94 | 49 | 30 | *(2144)* |
| First married | 56 | 93 | 61 | 44 | *(2581)* |
| Divorced with partner | 51 | 92 | 47 | 32 | *(95)* |
| **Parent status** | | | | | |
| Has children | 41 | 88 | 43 | 36 | *(2166)* |
| No children | 56 | 95 | 47 | 39 | *(6684)* |

**Standard of living better:** those who see their standard of living being about the same or better than other people's as opposed to judging it the same or worse.

**Feels in control of life:** those who feel that they had control over what happens to them in life (compared with those who felt they had no control).

**Satisfied with life:** those whose satisfaction with life puts them above the half way mark on the ten point scale (0 - 9) for all respondents, i.e. the point above which half the respondents marked the scale; this turned out to be 8.

**Belongs to a religion:** those who said they belonged to a particular religion (compared with those who had no religion).

Generally, the cohort members were very positive about their lives, especially with the control they felt they exercised over them. This focuses attention on the minority whose feelings were more negative. What characterised them?

Table 6.2 shows the percentages of cohort members expressing a positive view about themselves on the three self attitudes compared for different groups defined by gender, highest qualification, employment status, partnership status and parent status. With respect to gender, differences were very small. Women appeared, if anything, to have a more positive view of life than men; 48 per cent of women said they were satisfied with life compared with 43 per cent of men. This is particularly interesting because in many previous studies, women have tended to rate themselves less satisfied with life and less in control of events than men (e.g. Banks et al., 1992). It suggests that the changing behaviour among the young women of the 1970s generation, which has been charted in the preceding chapters, is matched by the increasing confidence and satisfaction reported here.

For highest qualification, much the same strong linear gradients we have seen throughout this and the earlier chapters were evident. Thus, perception of standard of living rose with rise in qualification, as did satisfaction with life. With respect to belief in control over life, the percentage feeling in control levelled at over 90 per cent for every qualification level above CSE level. But for those without qualifications it dropped to 82 per cent. Finally, employment status similarly showed quite strong relationships with these self attitudes. More unemployed people, and those in long term sickness, rated their standard of living *below* that of others. Those in employment rated their standard of living highest. Satisfaction with life followed a similar pattern: it was lowest for those with long-term sickness, and the unemployed, while those in full-time education, or in work, rated their satisfaction highest. People 'at home' (mostly women), fell in between. Finally, with respect to feeling in control over life, again the unemployed and the long-term sick had the lowest proportions saying they were - 70 per cent and 83 per cent respectively. This compared with 95 per cent of the groups in employment and in full-time education, and 88 per cent of people 'at home'.

Turning to partnership and parent status, there were similarly strong associations with the self attitudes. In the case of satisfaction with life and perceptions of a relatively high standard of living, for example, single people were least positive about their lives, and married people and cohabiting people the most positive. Those who were divorced were also *less* satisfied with life than those who were married. Having children was also associated with rather less satisfaction, and perceptions of a lower standard of living and less control over life.

These figures show another facet of the psychological state of cohort members, which we explored in the previous chapter by means of the *Malaise* inventory. The idea that 26-year-olds who are unemployed are as content with their lives as people in employment is refuted by the data. People in this state appeared far less happy with life. Similarly, women at home appeared to have less positive feelings about themselves than their counterparts in employment.

*Belonging to a religion*

The relationships between this aspect of personal identity and other variables were weaker than for the self attitudes, though fairly clear connections were still evident. As table 6.2 shows, substantially more female than male respondents (44 per cent compared with 32 per cent) said they belonged to a religion. Notably, in neither case was this a majority, underlining the tendency towards secularity in British society. Rather unexpectedly, religious affiliation was more common among those with qualifications above O' level than for others with qualifications at O' level or below. Only 27 per cent of those without any qualifications said they belonged to a religion. Among the unemployed, religious affiliation was lower than for those in employment, but this time those who were full-time students or were suffering from long term illness showed the highest levels of affiliation of all. Finally, married and single people were more likely to belong to a religion than were the cohabiting or the divorced. Parenthood appeared largely unconnected with religion.

We see in these findings indications of two kinds of need that religion may have been meeting. The first is more socially based and associated with the institution of marriage. The second is more personal and associated with suffering from long term sickness and living alone.

## Political involvement and preferences

The data on cohort members' attitudes illuminate their concerns both about key social issues and also their own situation. Another facet of their adult identities relates to politics. What did the cohort members think about the political system and what were their preferences within it? In this section, we examine two aspects of political orientation and activity: first, interest in politics and intention to vote in a general election; and second, party preferences. The cohort members were asked how interested they were in politics. They were also asked who they would vote for if there was a general election tomorrow. This included the option of saying that they would not vote at all. We examine the answers to these questions, comparing men and women, and then the relationship of the answers, first, to highest qualification, and second, to employment status. Again, there were few differences with respect to partnership status or parental status.

**Table 6.3    Interest in politics and voting preference: men and women in 1991 and 1996**

| Orientation | Men | | Women | |
|---|---|---|---|---|
| | **1991** | **1996** | **1991** | **1996** |
| **Interest** | % | % | % | % |
| Very interested | 11 | 8 | 3 | 3 |
| Fairly interested | 45 | 34 | 31 | 24 |
| Not very interested | 33 | 48 | 48 | 50 |
| No interest | 33 | 18 | 18 | 23 |
| | | | | |
| **Voting preference** | | | | |
| Not voting | 25 | 22 | 22 | 26 |
| Conservative | 33 | 23 | 36 | 18 |
| Labour | 28 | 37 | 27 | 37 |
| Lib/Dem | 11 | 9 | 12 | 13 |
| Other | 2 | 9 | 2 | 6 |
| *n (100%)* | *(4999)* | *(4078)* | *(5328)* | *(4496)* |

**Note:** 1991 percentages refer to 1958 cohort study members at age 33;
1996 percentages refer to 1970 cohort study members at age 26.

*Political interest and intention to vote*

Table 6.3 shows the percentages of male and female cohort members expressing different levels of interest in politics and their voting preference, including the intention not to vote. The comparative figures are also shown for the 1991 survey of the 1958 cohort. There was a noticeable decline between the two surveys in interest in politics. In 1991 just over half the men and one third of the women said they were interested ('fairly' or 'very'). In 1996 the proportions had dropped to 42 per cent men and 27 per cent women. This points to a substantial proportion of 26-year-olds who were relatively detached from politics. But this did not translate completely into an intention not to vote. About three quarters of men and a slightly smaller proportion of women indicated that they would vote - much the same percentages as in 1991.

As we might expect, interest in politics and intention to vote were strongly related to qualification level (Figure 6.6) and to employment status (Figure 6.7). Expression of interest in politics rose with qualification level, reaching over three fifths among people with degrees. This compared with less than one fifth interested among those without qualifications. Similarly, intention to vote rose with qualification level, but less sharply. Among those with no qualifications, three fifths said they would vote, compared with nearly four fifths of people with degrees. This differentiation was less marked for employment status. Cohort members classified as at home or permanently sick or disabled expressed the *least* interest in politics and, together with the unemployed, the *least* willingness to vote. Among employees, 77 per cent said they would vote. Among the permanently sick and disabled the proportions were down to 65 per cent and among people at home, 67 per cent.

**Figure 6.6  Interest in politics and intention to vote: compared for highest qualification groups**

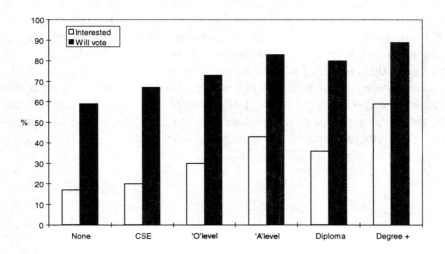

**Figure 6.7  Interest in politics and intention to vote: compared for employment status**

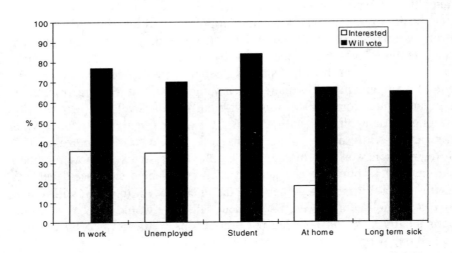

*Political preference*

Political preferences pointed to a surprising reversal over recent years. Analysis of voting figures in general elections has consistently pointed to majority Conservative support among women. (We found the same in the 1991 survey of the 1958 cohort.) However, among the 1970 cohort members questioned in 1996, preferences were reversed. Table 6.3 shows that over a third of both male and female cohort members favoured Labour and just over a fifth of men and just under a fifth of women supported the Conservatives. Compared with 1991, among women, support for the Conservatives appeared to have halved. Liberal Democrat support was nine per cent among men and 13 per cent among women.

**Figure 6.8  Voting preferences by highest qualification**

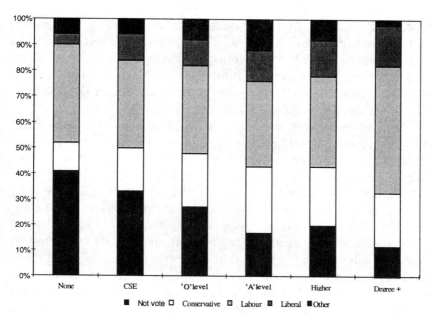

These voting preferences appeared in much the same form at all qualification levels and in all employment statuses. But exceptionally high Labour support was located, surprisingly, among those with degree level qualifications. Figure 6.8 shows that nearly half the cohort members in this category supported Labour, compared with just over a third in the other qualification groups. Conservative support never rose much above one quarter at any qualification level. Even more surprising was the general lack of Conservative support across all the employment status groups. Only among the full-time self-employed was there marginally more support for the Conservatives: 29 per cent Conservative, compared with 27 per cent Labour. Among all other groups Labour was in the majority. Among full-time employees, for example, there was 36 per cent support for Labour and 22 per cent for the Conservatives; among the unemployed, 46 per cent support for Labour and 9 per cent for the Conservatives.

There were signs that these trends had been accentuated since 1991, when the 1958 cohort study survey of 33-year-olds was carried out. Besides the radical shift in voting preferences, there were also marked signs of increasing disaffection, especially among the more marginalised groups. As with everything else, education seemed to underpin political involvement and participation. Lack of qualifications, unemployment and labour market inactivity went with disengagement.

## Values and identity

Expressions of attitudes to social issues, and the political system and political preferences, can be seen as expressions of deeper underlying values (Oppenheim, 1992). Moreover, there are common features of the more self-oriented expression of attitudes and affiliation which can be identified with dimensions of personality or *personal identity* (Banks et al., 1992). Can we find any evidence in our data for these?

To test whether any such more basic dimensions of attitude could be identified among the cohort members, a further factor analysis was undertaken, this time including the five attitude scales discussed earlier, the self attitude scales concerned with standard of living, control over life and life satisfaction, the expression of religion affiliation and the two expressions of political orientation - interest in politics and voting intention. The detailed results are given in Appendix 2.

Three factors emerged clearly, two of which could be identified with separate sets of more general values or *value dimensions*. The third appeared to be aligned more closely with a dimension of personal identity. All the original variables were associated with only one of the three dimensions, except support for the work ethic and religious affiliation which each spanned two of them.

*Political disaffection* comprised political cynicism, lack of interest in politics and intention not to vote. It was also associated, but more weakly, with *lack* of religious affiliation.

*Traditionalism* included support for law and order and support for traditional marital values. It also embraced, but more weakly, *support* for the work ethic and *opposition* to sex equality, and was associated with religious affiliation.

*Self efficacy* included satisfaction with life, belief that standard of living was relatively good and belief in ability to exercise control over life. It was also related, but more weakly, to *support* for the work ethic.

These dimensions are helpful in drawing out the main themes running through the findings presented in this chapter and the conclusions to be drawn from them.

First, we can see further evidence of the polarising processes to which the cohort members had been subjected - this time adding a value component to their more structurally based social inclusion or exclusion. Thus, both employment status and educational level particularly differentiated the attitudes held. Notably, those who were in the most marginalised groups, lacking in qualifications or unemployed or permanently sick, showed most *disaffection*. They were the most detached from the processes of citizenship, and the most cynical about politics.

Those in employment, or in full-time education, and especially those with the highest qualifications, were participating to the fullest extent. Underpinning their engagement was a high sense of *self efficacy*, embracing feelings of control and general satisfaction with life. Though there was less differentiation with respect to *traditionalism*, this too pointed to a less authoritarian stance on the part of those in higher education. Those who had achieved only a fairly minimum qualification, CSE, were the most traditional in their values, they supported tougher policies on law and order, were committed to the work ethic and opposed more sex equality. They were also more likely to have a religious affiliation.

So, in this last chapter we complete the circle begun earlier. A poor educational record restricts opportunities in the labour market, and in certain respects appears to speed up the transition to adulthood as reflected in family life. We now see that it may also lead to disengagement with citizenship as expressed through interest in politics and voting. Party preferences, too, show a growing disenchantment, if not with the Conservative Party as such, then certainly with the government of the day. We have to interpret the rise in support for Labour as reflecting the motivation for change.

# 7 Getting Somewhere, Getting Nowhere in the 1990s

JOHN BYNNER, ELSA FERRI and KATE SMITH

This book has focused on the theme 'getting on, getting by, getting nowhere'. Findings based on information collected in 1996 from nine thousand 26-year-olds have elaborated these themes in the main life domains for this cohort born in 1970. This includes their education and training; labour market experience; their partnerships and family life; health and health risks; and their attitudes and values. What have we learned? In this last chapter we try to reach some general conclusions about young adults in the 1990s. In doing so, we examine different types of lives, drawing on individual case records to provide summary 'pen portraits'. In addition, we examine some of the main features of continuity and change which the study has identified. To what extent are the old certainties about the course of life still in place in the 1990s, and how far are they being replaced by new structures or breaking down - perhaps irretrievably?

The second chapter of the book was concerned with education and qualifications, because of the centrality of these indicators of human and social *capital* in all of the areas of life that follow. However, since few people were still engaged in full-time education at age 26, this chapter does not examine education as an area of life in its own right. The focus is rather on employment, living arrangements, health and values.

People's jobs reflect, by and large, the education they have received, and this in turn reflects their family background. Up until the early 1970s, career paths and destinations were reasonably clear-cut. Those with higher education tended to fill the ranks of the professions; the two-thirds who left school at sixteen might expect to find employment, either via an apprenticeship in a 'skilled trade', or by direct entry into a job where extended training might or might not be provided. Young men's and young women's routes to becoming skilled were clearly demarcated, with boys tending to get the apprenticeships, and girls going to college for one year to get a secretarial or clerical qualification. The labour market was sufficiently accommodating to ensure that most people could find a place in it, either staying with the same employer, or moving from job to job, especially in the unskilled areas of work. With the new technology revolution of the 1970s, such certainties were reduced. As industry restructured massively, new types of jobs appeared, especially in the service sector, and large areas of traditional work disappeared.

The 1970 cohort members felt the brunt of these changes. The one in two who left school at 16 encountered a variety of training schemes to replace the youth jobs that were no longer on offer. Many became unemployed, living on the social security benefits for which they were still eligible at the time. Others were fortunate in getting jobs with good training attached. But how likely this was depended on the strength of the local labour market. In the prosperous South, the strong demand for labour meant there was usually little need to go on to a training scheme. In the declining industrial heartlands in the North and West, it was often the only option. By the time the cohort members were in their 20s the economy had recovered, but the new types of employment available demanded new types of skill. Some were able to take advantage of these opportunities. Others failed to make the adjustments necessary and were facing a future of casual unskilled work and unemployment.

These striking changes in employment prospects were paralleled by similar changes in personal and family life, characterised above all by diversity. A relatively large proportion of our cohort members were cohabiting, or had cohabited prior to marriage. Some had already separated, or were divorced. A substantial minority of both men and women had become parents by the age of 26; some, especially men, were not living with their own children; others were bringing up children who had been fathered by someone else. In contrast to those who had made the transition to a family life of their own, a sizeable number also remained unmarried or unpartnered, and a minority was still living at home with their parents. Others had adopted a single life style, living alone, or sharing accommodation with friends. The extended transition this represented gave these young people the opportunity to experiment with different kinds of jobs and lifestyles before making the longer term commitments that settling into marriage (or cohabitation) and parenthood entailed.

## Getting on

For those whose qualifications, skills and personal circumstances had enabled them to take advantage of the new occupational opportunities of the 1990s, their early years in the labour market had brought considerable success.

*Sophie's adjustment to the demands of the modern world appear to be rooted in her strong middle-class background. She gained the support she needed to complete a first degree and then a post graduate degree. She now works for a large company in a managerial position earning £20,000 a year. She is single, rents a flat with a friend and is in a relationship. She is strongly committed to 'sex equality', but has little interest in politics, believing that it doesn't make much difference which party is in power. Although she rates her health as excellent and does not smoke, she suffers from stress related symptoms such as stomach problems and indigestion.*

*Steve represents something of a 'loosening up' of the structures based on class and education, though he did not progress as far as Sophie in the education system. He stayed on at school until he was eighteen, collecting nine O' Levels and one A' Level, but then left to get a job. He is also employed in a large company where he earns an even higher salary of £30,000 a year. He lives in a flat of his own which he is buying with a mortgage. He is single and not in a relationship, has excellent health and feels very satisfied and in control of his life. Although he does not smoke, he does have a drink several times a week. He has no interest in politics and would not vote for any political party.*

Both of these individuals display the kinds of success that staying on in education brings, although to do so was likely to have required strong family support. Their lifestyles typify what was described in the eighties as 'Yuppy' - fast moving and successful, though, as Sophie's story shows, also bringing with it some stresses and strains. It is significant, too, that both Sophie and Steve had not made the transition to cohabitation or marriage, but had clearly invested much of their energy in advancing their careers.

*Getting by*

In contrast to these 'high fliers' in the labour market, those who had left school earlier, with relatively few qualifications, were likely to find themselves just 'getting by' in a job market characterised by insecurity, and demanding long hours of work for modest wages. Without further 'upskilling', it seemed likely that the future would hold only limited prospects for improvement. The young men and women in this situation were also likely to be married or in a partnership by the age of 26, and a considerable number had the further responsibilities of parenthood. Such responsibilities, often added to by the commitment of mortgage repayments, not only made heavy demands on modest earnings, but also constrained the opportunities for advancement in the labour market through mobility or further training.

*Barry has been in the same small company since leaving school at sixteen, and lives with his wife and four year old son in their own house. He and his wife lived together for four years, after which they got married. He has two children from a previous relationship, he has never been out of work and would rather have any job than be unemployed. He has four O' Levels, works in a skilled manual trade, involving supervision of six people and takes home £260 for a 55 hour week; his wife also works part-time. Although he says that he is not interested in politics and thinks that no political party has anything to offer him, he has strongly traditional and conservative views on certain topics. He believes that law and order should be strengthened, that the death penalty is appropriate for some crimes and that censorship should be extended. He is in good health but has a long standing health problem. He has given up smoking and drinks beer a couple of times a week.  He feels satisfied and in control of his life, thinking that his standard of living is better than that of other 26-year-olds.*

*Paul has been married to Sue for two years. They are buying their own home and have a young baby under a year old whom Sue looks after full-time. After leaving school at 17 with 5 CSEs and gaining a technical qualification Paul has had three full-time jobs. However, he has also had a couple of periods of unemployment, the longest being for between four and six months. Paul has been working in his current job doing skilled manual work for a year and he earns £250 for a 50 hour week. He is skilled at using tools and also in doing mathematical calculations and uses these skills at work. He rates his health as being good and does not suffer from any major health difficulties, although he has had a number of accidents and injuries since he was 16. Paul is reasonably satisfied with his life and thinks his standard of living is about the same as other people his age. He is fairly interested in politics and would vote Liberal Democrat. He also believes very strongly that marriage is for life.*

*Getting nowhere*

Now let us consider two 26-year-olds at the other end of the scale, both struggling to survive in the British society of the 1990s, and in many respects, *marginalised*. Leaving school at the minimum age without qualifications was followed by unskilled insecure jobs, coupled often with unemployment, early marriage and parenthood. Here, gender made a lot of difference, as men maintained the breadwinner role to try to get whatever jobs were available, while women frequently withdrew from the labour market to have and bring up children. Without a partner this meant living on social security benefits - often a near breadline existence - with few personal satisfactions to compensate for the material disadvantage felt. Although many would return to employment as their children got older, their lack of qualifications would restrict them to the kinds of cleaning jobs and unskilled manual work in factories to be found in the bottom of the labour market. Such jobs are, of course, usually poorly paid and highly insecure.

> **Darren** *is currently unemployed and has had a chequered employment career since leaving school at 16, having had seven full-time jobs and three part-time ones. He has also had five periods of unemployment - the longest of which was for over two years. He gained six CSEs at school (two of which were Grade 1) and has been on a number of Government training schemes - two being YTS. Darren does not feel he has many skills, particularly in writing and computing; however, he does rate his use of tools as fair. He lives alone in privately rented accommodation and is single, but in a relationship. Although he rates his health as good, Darren has suffered from a number of health problems since he was 16, including respiratory problems such as bronchitis and wheezing, persistent trouble with his mouth and pain in the back. He drinks lightly but does smoke about eight cigarettes a day. He is not interested in politics at all and would not vote - feeling strongly that politicians are only in politics for their own aims and none would do anything to benefit him. Darren's feelings about his life are not very positive - he thinks his standard of living is much worse than other 26-year-olds and does not feel in control of his life. He displays many symptoms of clinical depression and does not feel very satisfied with his situation.*

> **Paula** *is a divorced lone mother living in council housing with four children, the eldest aged seven, whom she gave birth to when she was in her teens. She left school at sixteen with two CSEs, does not currently*

*have a job, and is at home looking after the children. She rates her health as only fair, smokes about ten cigarettes every day and has a drink once or twice a week. She is not satisfied with her life and thinks that her standard of living is worse than that of most other people of her age. She feels that she does not have control over events and that nothing she does has any real effect on what happens to her. She also scores on the Malaise Scale as suffering from clinical levels of depression; she often feels miserable and depressed, and worries about things.*

The contrast with their peers who were 'getting on' could hardly have been greater than for those, such as Paula, who had become parents in their teens. The responsibility they held for supporting and bringing up children had accelerated their transition to adulthood. Yet in many respects, economically, they were in the weakest position to take it on. Many of these early parenting relationships had broken up, some through marital or cohabiting breakdown. The young women in this situation faced exceptional difficulties because reliance on state benefits, which had stayed at levels well below inflation, meant that they usually did not have access to the resources needed to make a success of family life. It was difficult to see how such young women would ever get out of the 'poverty trap'.

The six pen portraits presented above display the stratification of employment in modern Britain and how it impacts on many areas of life: pointing perhaps towards what has been described as the 30-30-40 society of the future (Hutton, 1995). While some were operating at the top of the scale, exhibiting occupational achievement as conventionally understood, others were getting by in routine work, while others again seemed to be trapped on the margins of the labour market, or outside it, in situations of insecurity and poverty. Although the numbers in serious difficulty at 26 were not large, all of the signs of *virtuous* and *vicious* circles were in place here, with those who had the family support, and education built on it, gaining access to good jobs, with high investment in them by employers; while others' situation worsened.

The economic high ground commanded by some, contrasting with the depths of economic disadvantage experienced by others, was paralleled by differentials in health. These were particularly noticeable in relation to measures of depression, and questions about control over life, satisfaction and self worth. The data consistently pointed to an accumulating set of disadvantages, beginning with poor educational achievement, and ending up with symptoms of poor psychological well-being and different kinds of illness. The only contradiction in this was the occasional evidence of depression at the upper end of the scale among those who were clearly finding the demands of 'high flier' employment too much.

Other cycles of more physically-based problems seemed to arise from, or to be set in motion by, disadvantage. Those who suffered from long term illness had missed out on educational and employment opportunities, increasing their sense of marginalisation and exclusion.

*Jill suffers from a long-term health problem and is currently experiencing a number of complaints. She rates her health as poor and suffers from migraine, persistent back pain, digestive trouble and problems with her bladder and kidneys. She has also suffered from depression and displays a number of clinical depression symptoms. Despite having left school at 16 with no qualifications, Jill has had a full-time job, although she has also experienced a number of periods out of the labour market due to her health and is currently not working but is long-term sick. She is single and not in a relationship, but lives at home with her parents. Jill drinks very lightly and has never smoked. She feels she is worse off than other people her age and does not feel in control of her life. She is also very unhappy with her situation.*

Others who started life in disadvantaged families were poorly educated, in low grade jobs and smoked more than the others, which itself placed them at greater risk of illness. Such a connection with poor health was not found for moderate drinking, indicating that this aspect of lifestyle was less clearly linked to economic position. In fact, people who never drank at all showed higher levels of depression than those who drank moderately, indicating that in the modern world for 26-year-olds complete lack of drinking may reflect a form of exclusion from social life.

In addition to the changes we have described in relation to the labour market and family life, much has been made recently of the perceived transformation of values in modern society. There has been widespread reference to what is seen as a significant rupture with the norms and values of the past. Our 26-year-olds, however, gave little evidence of this. Though they appeared very committed to the liberal standpoint of sex equality, in other respects their views tended more in a conservative or traditionalist direction. They were strong advocates of law and order, including capital punishment and censorship, and took, generally, a traditional standpoint on marriage and parenting. They were also committed to work, in the traditional

Protestant work ethic sense. They were cynical about politics and politicians, although high proportions still intended to vote.

Some movement in all these attitudes was also apparent, however, especially among the more educated. The more exposure to education that the cohort members had, the more generally liberal and less cynical they were. This extended into more positive views about themselves, their general life satisfaction, contentment with their standard of living, and sense of being in control of their lives. The more highly educated were also more positive about, and engaged with, the political process. In contrast, those who were unemployed, at home looking after their children, in part-time work, or unemployed, revealed a much higher degree of disaffection. They had little interest in politics and many indicated that they would not vote in a forthcoming election. Their exercise of 'citizenship' was often limited or non-existent.

Some important trends also emerged, however, in relation to voting preference. Another significant feature of the findings concerning these 26-year-olds, compared with our earlier survey of 33-year-olds conducted in 1991, was the substantial shift towards support for the Labour Party. This occurred among all groups, but particularly among women and the most educated. It may well be, however, that this was as much an expression of anti-government feeling, and a perceived 'need for change', as a deep-rooted ideological commitment.

## Continuities and discontinuities in young adulthood

The most striking features of the lives of our 26-year-olds lay in their similarities and dissimilarities to past generations. In comparison with their predecessors in the 1958 cohort, they represented a more polarised generation, with some gaining the benefits of extended education and human capital investment, while others were having more difficulty in getting by. There were signs that this gap was widening, an inevitable consequence of declining employment opportunities.

But perhaps more significant was the changing nature of employment itself. An ever higher premium was being placed on educational qualifications and a variety of skills in gaining access to the declining number of jobs on offer. In consequence, those young people who had left the education system at the earliest possible age were becoming increasingly disadvantaged later on. The staying-on rate in education had been rising steadily as the alternatives to unemployment in the labour market, especially youth training, had become increasingly stigmatised. It may well be that such an influx into education will do something to stem the tide towards social exclusion, but this has to be premised on an overall expansion of employment opportunities. Projections in such works as "The Jobless Future" (Aronowitz and DiFazio, 1995) suggest that this is unlikely. The more likely scenario is one of increasing numbers of people chasing fewer jobs. Permanent exclusion from all but the most marginal forms of job is, therefore, a real possibility for a growing number of people.

We have raised the question throughout this book as to what it is in people's lives that guarantees success and what, if anything, restricts it. In writing on the modern 'risk society', there has been much emphasis on the breaking down of the structural influences that determined the course of young people's lives in the past (Beck, 1986; Giddens, 1991). Our evidence on this is mixed. Rather against expectations, family background, as expressed by fathers' social class, still exercised strong influence on school achievements and occupational positions in adulthood. On the other hand, there was plenty of evidence of social mobility - a general loosening up of employment structures, giving many young people opportunities that perhaps would not have been open to them in the past. But this was almost certainly dependent upon taking advantage earlier on of extended educational opportunities, which was, of course, still dependent heavily on the kind of support they were getting at home. We have to conclude, therefore, that the structural influence of class on the transition to adulthood is still strongly in place.

If this is correct, our cohort members' lives may not be so different relatively from those with disadvantaged backgrounds in the past. Analysts of the effects of industrial change in Britain in the last century paint a graphic picture of the hardships brought about by technological change, which resonates with some of the findings we have presented here (e.g., Floud, 1997). Much of the reformist movements and politics then was about establishing humane means of helping families withstand unemployment and poverty. The difference today is that we have the comprehensive protective networks and institutions of the modern Welfare State; but these are coming under increasing strain. The fragility of marriage and personal relationships, together with the social and geographical fragmentation of the extended family, means that the lines of responsibility and support from this source can no longer be taken for granted. Furthermore, the social and economic protection furnished at a universal level by the Welfare State is increasingly contested as the emphasis on individual responsibility gains ground. We also have technological transformation accelerating on a scale, and at a pace, undreamed of in the past. Yet our ability to adapt our economic and social institutions in line with these changes lags dangerously far behind. In so far as our sample of 26-year-olds has lost people since the study began in 1970, it is from the less educated and more disadvantaged groups (Appendix 1). This suggests that, if anything, our data underestimate the extent of the problems the 1970 birth cohort faced.

With respect to gender, a more radical shift seemed to be occurring. Young women's opportunities at school and in the labour market were certainly enhanced over those of the previous generation. The strong commitment to equal opportunities, expressed through educational programmes of the 1980s, and resoundingly endorsed by the cohort members themselves, seemed to underpin a recognition of the need for improving women's economic position. Though this was still likely to change in response to having children, which often typically involved a move - at least temporarily - out of the labour market, there were strong signs that, over and above this, gender discrimination was reducing. Most of these benefits, of course, were seen at the upper end of the educational and occupational scales. The further down we move, the more gender differentiation becomes apparent. At the same time, another exceptionally disadvantaged group were young men who, through unemployment, were unable to provide economically for themselves, and certainly not for a family. Unmarried fathers, who had abdicated responsibility for their children, were one feature of this situation. A single life based on living at home with parents was another. The much higher levels of depression in these groups, male and female, pointed to an internalisation of their disadvantage at a higher level than in the past.

This takes us to the final conclusion of this book, the evidence of increasing polarisation and the accompanying attributes of anxiety, depression and even despair. If the 1970 cohort was moving into a 'post modern world', where all the old boundaries and certainties were breaking down, then this was something really being exploited only by those who had the human and social capital to succeed under the new conditions - and who would probably have done well under any circumstances. Marginalisation of others, locked into poor quality work, unemployment, poverty and disadvantage pointed more to the need for survival in the modern world, rather than to the transformation of society that the new and radical values were supposed to bring. These young people really were *getting nowhere* and nowhere is becoming a much harder place to be.

# Appendix 1
# Survey and Response
PETER SHEPHERD

## Introduction

The BCS70 1996 follow-up was conducted between April and September, 1996. A questionnaire developed by the Social Statistics Research Unit (SSRU) was mailed, by the MORI research organisation, to each member of the birth cohort for whom a current address was available. This Appendix reports on the design, development and conduct of the survey; and reviews the extent and nature of survey response.

## Questionnaire development

The questionnaire was developed by SSRU, in consultation with those who had been involved with the design and analysis of earlier BCS70 surveys, and those familiar with the National Child Development Study - the other birth cohort study for which SSRU is responsible, and based on a week's births in 1958. As the latest stage in a continuing study, it was vital that the questionnaire provide information that could be used in longitudinal analysis with data gathered during earlier follow-ups. It was also important that the information gathered provided an opportunity for comparison between the 1970 and 1958 birth cohorts.

To these ends, the questionnaire was designed to provide details of the views and current circumstances of the cohort member in a number of key areas; and more limited information on their experiences since the last follow-up in 1986. In order to encourage response, considerable efforts were made to keep the number of questions to a minimum, and to keep their form and wording as simple as possible so that they could be answered easily. Successive drafts of the questionnaire were piloted on groups of young people of approximately the same age as the cohort members, and the topics covered, question order, question form and wording subsequently amended.

In its final form the postal questionnaire was just sixteen pages in length, and included 51 questions concerning: education and training, qualifications and skills; employment and earnings; unemployment and periods out of the labour market; relationships, marriage and children; housing and household; health and health-related behaviour; and the views of cohort members about topics such as law and order, politics, jobs, and marriage and family.


## Tracing

The continued success of longitudinal studies like BCS70, is dependent on knowing the whereabouts of the study subjects. For the purposes of the follow-ups in 1975, 1980 and 1986, the cohort members were traced mainly through schools, and no effort was made to maintain contact in the intervening years. Following the 1986 survey, it was no longer possible to trace the 16,000 cohort members anew in this way, and after responsibility for the study was assumed by SSRU in 1991, efforts were made to maintain contact with those for whom a current address was still available, by mailing an annual birthday card. This was designed to give cohort members feedback about the use of information they had already given, and to advise them of plans for future surveys. It also provided an opportunity to confirm address details and other helpful information. As a result of these efforts, information about the current whereabouts of some 9,000 of the 16,000 BCS70 cohort members was available at the time that preparations for the 1996 follow-up began in January, 1996.

In an attempt to increase the number of current addresses, and thereby maximise response to the 1996 follow-up, a special tracing exercise was begun at that time. This was based on earlier, very successful, experience gained with tracing members of the 1958 cohort, but was more restricted in scope because of resource and time limitations. Sources of additional address information used during the tracing exercise included late returns to the 1995 birthday card, and early returns to the 1996 card which enabled confirmation and/or updating of existing information. Valuable address information was also obtained from a postal screening of the BCS70 cohort which was already underway as part of a study of inflammatory bowel disease, being carried out in collaboration with the Royal Free Hospital, London. This collaboration also enabled both projects to benefit from an approach to the Driver and Vehicle Licensing Agency, who agreed to mail tracing letters to cohort members identified by them on their address database. The administrative work at SSRU was carried out by a small tracing team, who also undertook tracing of cohort members for whom other methods failed. These efforts relied on information taken from BCS70 records, and required extensive use of the telephone, and the mailing of tracing letters. Latterly, after considerable work by Professor Neville Butler, it also proved possible to match many other untraced cohort members on the address records of the Family Health Service Authorities in England and Wales, and the Health Boards in Scotland.

This special tracing exercise ensured that throughout the first six months of 1996, there was a stream of information confirming and/or updating the information on the BCS70 address records. By the end of June 1996, information was available about the current whereabouts of an additional 4,500 cohort members and was already being used for the postal survey. A total of some 13,500 potential respondents were therefore available for the survey, leaving 2,500 cohort members whose whereabouts remained unknown.

## Survey

The survey was conducted between April and September, 1996. Questionnaires were mailed to all cohort members for whom a current address was available as a result of the tracing exercise described above. It was undertaken by the MORI research organisation who were responsible for the printing and distribution of questionnaires, the receipt of completed or returned questionnaires and the mailing of reminders.

Because of the nature of the tracing exercise described above, the mailing of questionnaires was carried out in three batches. The first, mailed in early April 1996, comprised all cohort members traced at that date through the birthday card, the Royal Free screening, the Driver and Vehicle Licensing Agency, and the other activities of the SSRU tracing team - some 9,803 individuals. The second, mailed in early May 1996, comprised all those cohort members newly traced by these same means - some 1,380 individuals. The third, mailed in early July, 1996 comprised again those newly traced, including for the first time those matched on the records of Family Health Service Authorities and Scottish Health Boards - some 2,291 individuals. All questionnaires were accompanied by a covering letter explaining the purpose of the survey.

For each batch, reminders were sent to those addresses for which there had been no response after 2-3 weeks. A second reminder was sent to those addresses from which there had still been no response after a further 3-4 weeks. The first reminder consisted of a letter only; the second included a further copy of the questionnaire.

As Table A1.1 shows, questionnaires were turned by 77 per cent of those mailed in the first batch - a very encouraging response. Response to batches two and three was less good, but this was perhaps not surprising, given that these cohort members include many who were traced for the first time in ten years. It is also possible that some of the address information was incomplete, inaccurate or out of date, especially that derived from the records of the Family Health Service Authorities and Scottish Health Boards. The table shows some direct evidence of this, and it is likely that these reasons also account for a large number of those for whom there was no response.

Overall, questionnaires were returned from two-thirds of those targeted.

## Table A1.1  Survey response

| Survey outcome | Batch 1* | | Batch 2 | | Batch 3 | | All | |
|---|---|---|---|---|---|---|---|---|
| | n | % | n | % | n | % | n | % |
| Fully complete questionnaire | 7382 | 75 | 666 | 48 | 750 | 33 | 8798 | 65 |
| Partially complete questionnaire | 172 | 2 | 20 | 2 | 13 | 1 | 205 | 2 |
| Refusal | 24 | <1 | 12 | 1 | 19 | 1 | 55 | <1 |
| Cohort member dead | 4 | <1 | 0 | - | 2 | <1 | 6 | <1 |
| Incomplete address | 0 | - | 0 | - | 2 | <1 | 2 | <1 |
| Other (cohort member away, etc) | 45 | 1 | 8 | 1 | 3 | <1 | 56 | <1 |
| No response to mailing | 2160 | 22 | 666 | 48 | 1478 | 65 | 4304 | 32 |
| Questionnaires mailed | 9803 | 100 | 1380 | 100 | 2291 | 100 | 13475 | 100 |

*Batch 1:    April, 1996 - All those traced by the birthday card, Royal Free screening, Driver and Vehicle Licensing Agency and the SSRU tracing team.

Batch 2:    May, 1996 - All those newly traced by the birthday card, Royal Free screening, Driver and Vehicle Licensing Agency and the SSRU tracing team.

Batch 3:    July, 1996 - All those newly traced by the birthday card, Royal Free screening, Driver and Vehicle Licensing Agency and the SSRU tracing team; plus those matched on Family Health Service Authority/Scottish Health Board records.

## Data preparation

Completed questionnaires were returned by cohort members to MORI, who were responsible for a preliminary visual edit agreed with SSRU. Following data entry of all pre-coded information, a preliminary computer edit (again agreed with SSRU) was carried out by MORI to check that data was valid (i.e. single-coded, 0-9), and within range (i.e. as specified in the questionnaire).

Following completion of the computer edit, all questionnaires were passed to another contractor, Eurodata, who carried out data entry of responses to open-ended questions, including reported qualifications, details of occupation, and health conditions. Qualifications were coded using a scheme based on that used for recent NCDS follow-ups, but because of an improved approach to the survey also provided information on each qualification identified. Occupation was coded using Computer-assisted Standard Occupational Coding (CASOC), developed by the Institute for Employment Research at the University of Warwick. This provides codings for the current standard occupational classification, socio-economic group, and social class, as well as other occupational classifications, such as KOS, CODOT, and Hope-Goldthorpe. Health conditions were coded using the International Classification of Diseases.

Unedited and edited data, together with all completed survey instruments, were subsequently passed to SSRU for further processing. This included: the coding of qualifications, occupation, and health data; further computer editing to ensure that data were consistent; establishment of a clean and documented cross-sectional data base to facilitate the early analysis reported here; and linking of the new sample survey data with that from earlier BCS70 follow-ups to establish a longitudinal data base to permit more detailed longitudinal analysis, including the response analysis reported in this Appendix.

## Response bias

Although a generally acceptable response rate has been achieved, anything less than a perfect response raises the question of whether those who completed a questionnaire are representative of the sampled population - in this case, the cohort members living in Great Britain (England, Wales and Scotland) for whom SSRU had a current address. This issue has been explored by exploiting a possibility only available to longitudinal studies: comparison of the achieved sample - those cohort members who returned a questionnaire - with the target sample - the cohort at birth, and in subsequent follow-ups.

Comparisons between the achieved sample and the target sample have been extensive. They are based on variables selected from the earlier BCS70 follow-ups. The variables chosen include many relating to demography, education, literacy and numeracy problems, social and economic circumstances, financial problems, the family and relationships, housing and household, and health.

Table A1.2 reports on just some of the comparisons made. It contrasts the characteristics of the target sample and those of the achieved sample for the 1996 follow-up, using a range of variables selected to represent the areas identified above. The absolute difference between the target and achieved samples, and the percentage bias are reported for each variable, indicating the extent of the difference between the cohort and the sample. For this table percentage bias is calculated as follows:

*((Per cent in the achieved sample - Per cent in the target population)/Per cent in the target population) x 100*

A negative percentage bias indicates under-representation in the 1996 follow-up, and a positive percentage bias shows over-representation. When looking at the contrasts for variables taken from the 1975, 1980, and 1986 follow-ups it is important to remember that the target percentage will itself reflect differential response to these surveys.

Nevertheless, the analysis provides an important, and generally encouraging, insight into differential response. Absolute differences between the sampled population and the achieved sample are, on the whole, small and this is reflected in many of the figures for percentage bias. However, small absolute differences can result in a relatively large figure for percentage bias where the percentage in the sampled population is small. Levels of statistical significance are not reported, but it should be noted that, in samples of this size, tests of statistical significance are sensitive to very small differences. In general, the achieved sample does not differ greatly from the sampled population.

Overall, it appears that men, those born outside Britain, and those with minority ethnic background are under-represented in the BCS70 1996 follow-up. This also holds for those born to single mothers, teenage mothers, and unemployed fathers; as well as for those with low school achievement; those with a disability, those who have been in care, those with origins in the lower social classes, those who grew-up in families with financial problems, and those who have experienced poor housing conditions.

Perhaps not surprisingly, this picture is similar to that emerging from the analyses of differential response to other surveys, and especially the NCDS follow-ups.

Finally, it is important to note that this analysis of differential response reveals that those reporting problems with reading, writing and mathematics at school are under-represented in the achieved sample for the 1996 follow-up survey. This is an unavoidable consequence of the postal survey method.

**Table A1.2    Response bias - comparison with earlier BCS70 follow-ups**

| | Target % | Achieved % | Difference % | Bias % |
|---|---|---|---|---|
| Male respondents | 51.1 | 45.6 | -5.5 | -10.76 |
| *1970 Birth Survey* | | | | |
| Mother born outside Britain | 8.1 | 6.8 | -1.3 | -16.05 |
| Father born outside Britain | 8.7 | 7.1 | -1.6 | -18.39 |
| Mother completed education aged less than 15 years | 5.9 | 6.3 | +0.4 | +6.78 |
| Father completed education aged less than 15 years | 7.6 | 6.9 | -0.7 | -9.21 |
| Teenage mother | 8.7 | 7.9 | -0.8 | -9.20 |
| Single mother | 4.1 | 3.5 | -0.6 | -14.63 |
| Premarital conception | 8.1 | 7.8 | -0.3 | -3.70 |
| Twin at birth | 2.0 | 1.9 | -0.1 | -5.00 |
| Father's social class - Manual | 64.1 | 61.6 | -2.5 | -3.90 |
| Father unemployed | 3.0 | 2.5 | -0.5 | -16.67 |
| | | | | |
| *1975 Follow-up* | | | | |
| Child's ethnic group - West Indian | 1.0 | 0.7 | -0.3 | -30.00 |
| Parents have no educational qualifications | 38.0 | 34.7 | -3.3 | -8.68 |
| Mother aged over 40 years | 2.3 | 2.1 | -0.2 | -8.70 |
| Child living with both natural parents | 91.5 | 92.5 | +1.0 | +1.09 |
| Mother and child ever separated for one month or more | 4.5 | 3.9 | -0.6 | -13.33 |
| Father's social class - Manual | 63.1 | 60.2 | -2.9 | -4.60 |
| Weighed under 5lbs at birth | 6.5 | 6.1 | -0.4 | -6.15 |
| No congenital abnormality | 93.2 | 92.9 | -0.3 | -0.32 |
| No disability | 93.8 | 93.9 | +0.1 | +0.11 |
| Family has moved 3 or more times since 1970 | 9.8 | 9.1 | -0.7 | -7.14 |
| Accommodation is crowded (> 1 person/room) | 16.5 | 14.4 | -2.1 | -12.73 |
| Accommodation rented privately | 5.0 | 4.8 | -0.2 | -4.00 |
| Social rating of neighbourhood - Poor | 5.8 | 5.1 | -0.7 | -12.07 |

*continued* ............

| continued ...... | Target | Achieved | Difference | Bias |
|---|---|---|---|---|
| | % | % | % | % |
| **1980 Follow-up** | | | | |
| Has great difficulty with mathematics | 3.6 | 3.1 | -0.5 | -13.89 |
| Has great difficulty with reading | 3.1 | 2.4 | -0.5 | -22.58 |
| Has great difficulty with writing | 2.4 | 2.2 | -0.2 | -8.33 |
| Child has lived with the same parents since birth | 87.3 | 88.3 | +1.0 | +1.15 |
| Child has lived with only one parent | 15.9 | 14.6 | -1.3 | -8.18 |
| Child living in residential institution | .6 | .5 | -0.1 | -16.67 |
| Father's social class - Manual | 52.5 | 50.1 | -2.4 | -4.57 |
| Family receives Supplementary Benefit | 8.4 | 7.2 | -1.2 | -14.29 |
| Has a disability | 7.6 | 7.2 | -0.4 | -5.26 |
| Child has never smoked | 74.6 | 75.8 | +1.2 | +1.61 |
| Family lived at 4+ places since 1975 | 13.3 | 13.2 | -0.1 | -0.75 |
| Accommodation rented privately | 3.0 | 2.7 | -0.3 | -10.00 |
| | | | | |
| **1986 Follow-up** | | | | |
| Child born outside Britain | 2.3 | 2.0 | -0.3 | -13.04 |
| Pupil's reading ability impaired | 8.1 | 4.9 | -3.2 | -39.51 |
| Child assessed as top of academic ability range | 5.4 | 6.2 | +0.8 | +14.81 |
| Child wishes to stay at school to take 'A' levels | 45.7 | 48.0 | +2.3 | + 5.03 |
| Child lives with natural parents | 81.7 | 82.2 | +0.5 | +0 .61 |
| Child has been "in care" | 1.3 | 1.0 | -0.3 | -23.08 |
| Child wants to leave home as soon as possible | 5.2 | 4.6 | -0.6 | -11.54 |
| Father's social class - Manual | 49.0 | 47.6 | -1.4 | -2.86 |
| Family receives Supplementary Benefit | 11.2 | 9.6 | -1.6 | - 14.29 |
| Has disability | 9.5 | 7.6 | -1.9 | - 20.00 |
| Child does not smoke | 79.2 | 79.7 | +0.5 | +0 .63 |
| Four+ addresses since 1980 | 1.7 | 1.4 | -0.3 | -17.65 |
| Accommodation is rented privately | 2.7 | 2.9 | +0.2 | + 7.41 |

Target % = Per cent in BCS70.    Achieved % = Per cent in achieved sample.
Difference = Target %-Achieved %.    Bias % = ((Achieved % - Target %)/Target %) x 100.

# Appendix 2
# Factor Analysis of Attitude Variables

JOHN BYNNER and DICK WIGGINS

Two factor analyses, using the SPSS computer package, were carried out on the opinion data presented in Chapter 6. Each involved first the computation of a product moment correlation matrix using 'list-wise' deletion of missing cases. This was followed by a principal components analysis and then a Varimax (orthogonal) rotation of all factors with latent roots greater than 1. Varimax rotation was followed by oblique rotation (i.e. allowing the factors to be correlated) using the Oblimin method.

The first factor analysis was carried out on the 17 opinion variables. Five factors were identified. The factor loadings for the oblique Oblimin solution are shown in Table A2.1. Highest factor loadings, which were used to define each factor and determine a label for it, are shown in bold in Table A2.1. The only anomalous loading was for *support for the work ethic*, which received only one high loading and linked the 'left-right' item 16 rather inappropriately to the factor (it was not used to measure the factor).

The second factor analysis was carried out on the correlations among the five attitude factors, the three self attitude variables, the religious affiliation variable and the political orientation variables (interest and voting intention).

Three factors were obtained. The Oblimin solution failed to converge, suggesting that only an orthogonal Varimax solution was appropriate, i.e. there was no correlation among the factors. The factor loadings for the Varimax solution are shown in Table A2.2. Highest factor loadings, which were used to define each factor and determine a label for it, are shown in bold in Table A2.2.

Finally, Table A2.3 shows the means, standard deviations and reliability coefficients (Cronbach's alpha) for each of the scales used to measure each of the five attitude factors. The factor scores for the first set of factors were obtained by averaging the scores on the individual scales used to define each factor. These were the scores used to produce Figures 2.1 to 2.5 in Chapter 6. Notably, all the scales showed much the same variability in the scores as shown by the standard deviations, except for *support for sex equality*, where the variability was much less. The most reliable scales were political cynicism and support for traditional marital values, with reliability coefficients over .60. The least reliable scale was support for the work ethic - reliability coefficient, .40. This latter scale ideally needs more items to be measured reliably.

### Table A2.1  Factor analysis of opinion variables: factor loadings

| | Law and order | Political cynicism | Sex equality | Marital values | Work ethic |
|---|---|---|---|---|---|
| 1 The law should be obeyed even if a particular law is wrong | **.40** | .16 | .02 | -.09 | .30 |
| 2 There should be more women bosses in important jobs in business and industry | .04 | .03 | **.73** | -.02 | -.13 |
| 3 Having almost any job is better than being unemployed | .08 | -.13 | .01 | -.16 | **.70** |
| 4 For some crimes the death penalty is the most appropriate sentence | **.70** | .25 | -.12 | .10 | .04 |
| 5 When both partners work full-time, the man should take an equal share of domestic chores | .12 | -.05 | **.68** | .05 | .12 |
| 6 It does not make much difference which political party is in power in Britain | .02 | **-.71** | .03 | .02 | .13 |
| 7 Divorce is too easy to get these days | .21 | -.02 | .01 | **-.65** | .03 |
| 8 If I didn't like a job I'd pack it in even if there was no other job to go to | -.08 | .02 | .05 | -.08 | **.37** |
| 9 Marriage is for life | -.03 | .11 | .05 | **-.73** | .23 |
| 10 Politicians are mainly in politics for their own benefit and not for the benefit of the community | -.02 | **-.72** | -.02 | -.01 | -.08 |
| 11 Censorship of films and magazines is necessary to uphold moral standards | **.59** | .21 | .16 | -.21 | -.15 |
| 12 Men and women should all have the chance to do the same kind of work | .01 | .03 | **.72** | -.01 | -.01 |
| 13 None of the political parties would do anything to benefit me | .12 | **-.81** | .02 | -.03 | -.02 |
| 14 People who break the law should be given stiffer sentences | **.72** | .16 | .06 | .00 | .08 |
| 15 Couples who have children should not separate | -.05 | -.09 | -.20 | **-.72** | .03 |
| 16 Government should redistribute income from the better off to those who are less well off | .25 | .23 | -.24 | .34 | **.34** |
| 17 If a child is ill and both partners are working it should usually be the mother who takes time off work to look after the child | -.26 | .00 | **.43** | .25 | .19 |

**Table A2.2 Factor analysis of social attitudes, self attitudes, religious and political orientation variables: factor loadings**

| | Factors | | |
|---|---|---|---|
| | **Disaffection** | **Efficacy** | **Traditionalism** |
| Support for sex equality | -.05 | .20 | **-.40** |
| Support for law and order | .22 | .18 | **.68** |
| Support for traditional marital values | -.01 | .01 | **.69** |
| Political cynicism | **.68** | -.20 | .05 |
| Support for the work ethic | .02 | **.42** | **.47** |
| Belongs to a religion | **-.42** | .08 | **.43** |
| Standard of living | -.02 | **.68** | .05 |
| Feels in control of life | .02 | **.58** | -.16 |
| Satisfaction with life so far | .07 | **.72** | .05 |
| Political interest | **-.75** | -.03 | -.19 |
| Intends to vote | **-.73** | -.01 | .02 |

**Table A2.3 Statistics for social attitude scales**

| | **Mean score** | **Standard deviation** | **Reliability coefficient** |
|---|---|---|---|
| Political cynicism | 2.94 | .75 | .65 |
| Support for sex equality | 3.99 | .55 | .55 |
| Support for law and order | 3.65 | .70 | .54 |
| Support for traditional marital values | 3.29 | .74 | .61 |
| Support for work ethic | 3.43 | .74 | .40 |

# References

Arnetz, B.B., Brenner, S.O., Levi, L., Hjelm, R., Petterson, I.L., Wasserman, J., Petrini, B., Eneroth, P., Kallner, A., Kvetnansky, R. and Vigas, M. (1991), Neuroendocrine and Immunological Effects of Unemployment and Job Insecurity. *Psychotherapy and Psychosomatics* 55: 76-80.

Ashton, D. and Maguire, M. (1986), *Young Adults in the Labour Market.* Department of Employment Research Paper, No 55, London: Department of Employment.

Banks, M., Bates, I., Breakwell, G., Bynner, J., Emler, N., Jamieson, L. and Roberts, K. (1992), *Careers and Identities*, Buckingham: Open University Press.

Banks, M. and Ullah, P. (1988), *Youth Unemployment in the 1980s: its Psychological Effects*, Beckenham, Croom Helm.

Bartley, M.J., Blane, D. and Montgomery, S.M. (1997), Health and the life course: why safety nets matter. *British Medical Journal*, 314: pp 1194-1196.

Bates, I., Clarke, J., Cohen, P., Finn, D., Moore, R. and Willis, P. (1984), *Schooling for the Dole*, London: MacMillan.

Beck, U. (1986), *Risk Society*, London: Sage.

Becker, G.S. (1975), *Human Capital*. Washington DC: National Bureau of Economic Research.

Bosello, O., Zamboni, M., Armellini, F. and Todesco, T. (1993), Biological and clinical aspects of regional body fat. *Diabetes, Nutrition and Metabolism* 6: 163-171.

Buck, N., Gershuny, J., Rose, D. and Scott, J. (1994), *Changing Households: the British Household Panel Survey 1990-1992*, ESRC Research Centre on Microsocial Change, University of Essex.

Burghes, L. (1993), *One Parent Families: Policy Options for the 1990s*, Joseph Rowntree Foundation.

Burghes, L. with Brown, M. (1995), *Single Lone Mothers: Problems, Prospects and Policies*, Joseph Rowntree Foundation.

Butler, N.R. and Bonham, D.G. (1963), *Perinatal Mortality*, Edinburgh: Livingstone.

Bynner, J. (1991), 'Transition to Work: Results from a Longitudinal Study of Young People in four British Labour Markets', in Ashton, D. and Lowe, G. (eds), *Making their Way: A Comparison between Educational, Training and the Labour Market in Canada and Britain*. Milton Keynes: Open University Press.

Bynner, J. (1996), 'Resisting Youth Unemployment: the Role of Education and Training' in De Goede, M.P.M., Klaver, P.M., Van Ophem, J.A.C., Verhaar, C.H.A. and de Vries, A., *Youth: Unemployment, Identity and Policy.* Aldershot: Avebury.

Bynner, J. (forthcoming), 'New Routes to Employment: Integration and Exclusion', in Heinz, W.R. (ed), *From Education to Work: Cross-national Perspectives*, Cambridge University Press.

Bynner, J. and Ashford, S. (1994), Politics and Participation: Some Antecedents of Young People's Attitudes to the Political System and Political Activity, *European Journal of Sociology* 24, pp. 223-36.

Bynner, J. and Fogelman, K. (1993), 'Making the Grade: Education and Training Experiences', in Ferri, E. (ed), *Life at 33*. London: National Children's Bureau.

Bynner, J., Morphy, L. and Parsons, S. (1996), *Women, Employment and Skills*, NCDS User Support Group Working Papers, No 43, SSRU, City University.

Bynner, J. and Roberts, K. (eds) (1991), *Youth and Work*, London: Anglo German Foundation.

Bynner, J. and Steedman, J. (1995), *Difficulties with Basic Skills*, London: Basic Skills Agency.

Chamberlain, R., Chamberlain, G., Howlett, B.C and Claireaux, A. (1975), *British Births*, London: Heinemann.

Clarke, M. (1978), The unemployed on supplementary benefit: living standards and making ends meet on a low income. *Journal of Social Policy* 7: 385-410.

Davie, R., Butler, N.R. and Goldstein, H. (1972), *From Birth To Seven*, London: Longman in association with National Children's Bureau.

DfEE (Department for Education and Employment) (1997), 'Women in the Labour Market: results from the Spring Labour Force Survey', *Labour Market Trends*, 105, 3, pp. 99-120.

Douglas, J.W.B. (1964), *The Home and the School*, London: MacGibbon and Kee.

Ekinsmyth, C. and Bynner, J.(1994), *The Basic Skills of Young Adults*, London: Basic Skills Agency.

Ekinsmyth, C., Bynner, J., Montgomery, S. and Shepherd, P. (1992), An integrated approach to the design and analysis of the 1970 British Cohort Study (BCS70) and the National Child Development Study (NCDS), *SSRU Cohort Studies Working Paper*, No. 1, Social Statistics Research Unit, City University.

Evans, K. and Furlong, A. (1996), 'Metaphors of Youth Transitions: Niches, Pathways, Trajectories and Navigations' in Bynner, J., Chisholm, L. and Furlong, A. (eds), *Youth Citizenship and Social Change*, Aldershot: Ashgate.

Ferri, E. (ed) (1993), *Life At 33: The Fifth Follow-up of the National Child Development Study*, London: National Children's Bureau.

Ferri, E. and Smith, K. (1996), *Parenting in the 1990s*, London: Family Policy Studies Centre.

Floud, J.E., Halsey, A.H. and Martin, F.M. (1956), *Social Class and Educational Opportunity*, London: Heinemann.

Floud, R. (1997), *The People and the British Economy: 1830-1914*, Oxford University Press.

Fogelman, K. (1976), *Britain's Sixteen-year-olds*, London: National Children's Bureau.

Galbraith, J.K. (1992), *The Politics of Contentment*, London: Sinclair Stevenson.

Giddens, A. (1992), *Modernity and Self-Identity*, Cambridge: Polity Press.

Gittleman, M. (1994), Earnings in the 1980s: An Occupational Perspective, *Monthly Labour Review*, July.

Glyn, A. (1995), The Assessment: Unemployment and Inequality, *Oxford Review of Economic Policy* 11, No 1: 1-25.

Grant, G., Nolan, M. and Ellis, N. (1990), A reappraisal of the Malaise Inventory. *Social Psychiatry and Psychiatry. Epidemiol* 25: 170-178.

Green, F. (1994), 'Training, Inequality and Inefficiency' in Glyn, A. and Miliband, D. (eds), *Paying for Inequality*, London: Rivers Oram.

Gregg, P. and Wadsworth, J. (1996), 'More work in fewer households?' in Hills (ed.), *New Inequalities: The Changing distribution of income and wealth in the United Kingdom*, pp. 181-207, Cambridge: Cambridge University Press.

Hall, R. (1997), The Changing Geography of Living Alone: Evidence from England and Wales and France for the Last Two Decades, *Paper presented to ESRC Dissemination Conference on Population and Household Change Programme*.

Halsey, A.H., Heath, A.F. and Ridge, J.M. (1980), *Origins and Destinations: Family and Class Education in Modern Britain*, Oxford: Clarendon Press.

Haskey, J. (1992), Pre-marital Cohabitation and the Probabilities of Subsequent Divorce: Analyses Using New Data from the General Household Survey, *Population Trends*, 68. OPCS/HMSO.

Heath, A. and Topf, R. (1987), 'Political Culture in British Social Attitudes', in Jowell, R., Witherspoon, S. and Brook, L. (eds), *British Social Attitudes Survey: the 1987 Report*, Aldershot: Gower.

Hills, J. (1996), 'Introduction: after the turning point' in Hills (ed.), *New Inequalities: The Changing distribution of income and wealth in the United Kingdom*, Cambridge: Cambridge University Press.

Hutton, W. (1995), *The State We're In*, London: Cape.

Johnson, P. and Reed, H. (1996), *Two Nations? The Inheritance of Poverty and Affluence*, Institute for Fiscal Studies, London.

Jones, G. (1995), *Leaving Home*, Buckingham: Open University Press.

Joshi, H. E. and Newell, M-L. (1989), *Pay Differentials and Parenthood: Analysis of men and women born in 1946*. Coventry: Institute of Employment Research, Warwick University.

Kaplan, H.B. (1991), Social Psychology of the Immune System: A Conceptual Framework and Review of the Literature. *Soc Sci Med* 33: 909-23.

Kiernan, K. (1995), *Transition to Parenthood: Young Mothers, Young Fathers - Associated Factors and Later Life Experiences*, London: STICERD, London School of Economics.

Kiernan, K. (1997), Who Divorces?, *Paper presented to ESRC Dissemination Conference on Population and Household Change Programme*.

Kiernan, K. and Estaugh, V. (1993), *Cohabitation: Extra-marital Childbearing and Social Policy*, Occasional paper 17, Family Policy Studies Centre.

Kline, P. (1994), *An Easy Guide to Factor Analysis*, London: Routledge.

Macran, S., Joshi, H.E. and Dex, S. (1996), 'Employment After Childbearing: a Survival Analysis', accepted by *Work, Employment and Society*. Vol. 10, 2, (273-296).

Marsh, A. (1990), *Political Action in Europe and the USA*, London: MacMillan.

McKennell, A. (1977), 'Attitude measurement', in O'Muircheartaigh, C.A. and Payne, C. (eds), *The Analysis of Survey Data*, Volume II, Chapter 7, London: John Wiley.

McRae, S. (1993), *Cohabiting Mothers: Changing Marriage and Motherhood?*, Policy Studies Institute.

Montgomery, S.M. (1996), *The relationship of unemployment with  health and health behaviour in young men*. PhD thesis, The City University, London.

Montgomery, S.M., Bartley, M.J., Cook, D.G. and Wadsworth, M.E.J. (1995), Are young unemployed men at greater risk of future illness, even before they experience any unemployment?, *Journal of Epidemiology and Community Health* 49: 552.

Montgomery, S.M., Bartley, M.J., Cook, D.G. and Wadsworth, M.E.J. (1996), Health and social precursors of unemployment in young men in Great Britain. *Journal of Epidemiology and Community Health* 50:415-422.

Montgomery, S.M., Bartley, M.J., Cook, D.G. and Wadsworth, M.E.J. (forthcoming), Unemployment, cigarette smoking, alcohol consumption and body weight in young British men. *European Journal of Public Health*.

Nickell, S. and Bell, B. (1995), The Collapse in Demand for the Unskilled and Unemployment Across the OECD. *Oxford Review of Economic Policy* 11, no 1: 40-62.

Office of Population Censuses and Surveys (1994), *1992 Marriage and Divorce Statistics: England and Wales*, HMSO. *Social Trends 1996*, London: HMSO.

Oppenheim, A. N. (1992), *Questionnaire Design, Interviewing and Attitude Measurement*, London: Pinter.

Paci, P. and Joshi, H. (1996), *Wage Differential Between Men and Women: Evidence from the Cohort Studies*, Research Report 71, Department for Education and Employment.

Payne, J., Payne, C. and Connolly, S. (1994), Long-term Unemployment: Individual Risk  Factors and Outcomes (An Analysis of Data from the National Child Development Study). *Report to the Employment Department from the Policy Studies Institute* (Unpublished).

Pilling, D. (1990), *Escape from Disadvantage*, London: The Falmer Press.

Richman, N. (1978), Depression in mothers of young children. *Journal of the Royal Society of Medicine*, 71:489-493.

Rutter, M., Tizard, J. and Whitmore, K. (1970), *Education, Health and Behaviour*, London: Longman.

Schoon, I. and Montgomery, S.M. (forthcoming), Zum Zusammenhang frühkindlicher Lebenserfahrungen und Depression im Erwachsenenalter. *Zeitschrift für Psychosomatische Medizin und Psychoanalyse*.

Utting, D. (1995), *Family and Parenthood: Supporting Families, Preventing Breakdown*, Joseph Rowntree Foundation.

Wadsworth, M.E.J. (1991), *The Imprint of Time: Childhood History and Adult Life* Oxford: Clarendon Press.

Ward, C., Dale, A. and Joshi, H.E. (1993), Participation in the Labour Market, in E. Ferri (ed), *Life at 33: The Fifth Follow-up of the National Child Development Study*, London: National Children's Bureau, pp. 60-91.

White, M.(1991), *Against Unemployment*, London: Policy Studies Institute.

Wiggins, R.D. and Bynner, J. (1993), Social Attitudes, in Ferri, E. (ed), *Life at 33: The Fifth Follow-up of the National Child Development Study*, London: National Children's Bureau.

Wilkinson, H. (1994), *No Turning back: Generations and the Genderquake*, London: Demos.

Wilkinson, R.G. (1996), *Unhealthy Societies*, London: Routledge.

# Index